FROM

BRETTON WOODS

TO

REGNERY GATEWAY — CHICAGO

WORLD INFLATION

A STUDY OF
CAUSES AND CONSEQUENCES

Henry Hazlitt

Reprinted 2009 by the Ludwig von Mises Institute
Auburn, Alabama

Second printing prepared with the kind permission of the Foundation for Economic Educati

Published by Regnery Gateway, Inc.
360 West Superior Street
Chicago, Illinois 60610

Library of Congress Cataloging in Publication Data
Hazlitt, Henry, 1894-
  From Bretton Woods to world inflation.

  1. International finance—Addresses, essays, lectures. 2. United
Nations Monetary and Financial Conference (1944: Bretton Woods,
N. H.)—Addresses, essays, lectures. 3. International Monetary
Fund—Addresses, essays, lectures. 4. Inflation (Finance)—Addresses,
essays, lectures. I. Title.
HG3881.H36 1983   332.4'566   83-43042   ISBN 0-89526-617-2

Manufactured in the United States of America.

CONTENTS

Part II: The Aftermath

Introduction

The purpose of this book is to re-examine the consequences of the decisions made by the representatives of the forty-five nations at Bretton Woods, New Hampshire, forty years ago. These decisions, and the institutions set up to carry them out, have led us to the present world monetary chaos. For the first time in history, every nation is on an inconvertible paper money basis. As a result, every nation is inflating, some at an appalling rate. This has brought economic disruption, chronic unemployment, and anxiety, destitution, and despair to untold millions of families.

It is not that inflation had not occurred before the Bretton Woods Conference in July, 1944. Inflation's widespread existence at the time, in fact, was the very reason the conference was called. But at that meeting, chiefly under the leadership of John Maynard Keynes of England, all the wrong decisions were made. Inflation was institutionalized. And in spite of the mounting monetary chaos since then, the world's political officeholders have never seriously re-examined the inflationist assumptions that guided the authors of the Bretton Woods agreements. The main institution set up at Bretton Woods, the International Monetary Fund, has not only been retained, its inflationary powers and practices have been enormously expanded.

Yet this book would never have been put together had it not been for the encouragement and initiative of my friends, Elizabeth B. Currier, Executive Vice President of the Committee for Monetary Research & Education, and George Koether. We were talking about the current world monetary chaos, and one of them referred to the possible role played by the monetary system set up at Bretton Woods. I happened to remark that when the conference was taking place I was an editor on *The New York Times*, that I was writing nearly all its editorials on the Bretton Woods decisions as they were being daily reported, and that in them I was constantly calling attention to the inflationary consequences those successive decisions would lead to.

Both Mr. Koether and Mrs. Currier immediately suggested that it might serve a useful purpose to reprint some of these editorials now. I told them I had long ago sent my *New York Times* scrapbooks, together with other papers, to the George Arents Research Library in Syracuse University, and that the scrapbooks were the only place I knew of where these editorials had been identified as mine. George Koether undertook to make the trip to Syracuse, studied the scrapbooks, and sent me photostats of 26 of them. The thoroughness of his research is shown by the fact that these included not only *Times* editorials of mine which appeared between June 1, 1944 and April 7, 1945, but one that was published on the virtues of the gold standard on July 9, 1934. His discrimination was such that I am confident he did not miss a single essential comment. Of the 26 editorials he sent, I am reprinting 23. I am greatly in debt to his selective judgment.

I feel that these editorials do warrant republication at this time, not to prove that my misgivings turned out to be justified, but to show that if sound economic and monetary understanding had prevailed in 1945 at Bretton Woods, and in the American Congress and Administration, these inflationary consequences would have been recognized, and the Bretton Woods proposals rejected.

When I began to re-read these old *New York Times* editorials I was reminded that I had summarized all the misgivings expressed in them in an article in *The American Scholar* of Winter, 1944/5, under the title "The Coming Economic World Pattern: Free Trade or State Domination?" I republish that here also. And once I had begun the brief history that follows of the actual workings of the Bretton Woods institutions, particularly The International Monetary Fund, I decided to include five other pieces: (1) excerpts from my book *Will Dollars Save The World?* which appeared in 1947; (2) a column in *Newsweek* magazine of Oct. 3, 1949, on the devaluation of the British pound and twenty-five other world currencies in the two weeks preceding; (3) my column for the *Los Angeles Times* Syndicate, Nov. 21, 1967, "Collapse of a System;" (4) another column for the *Los Angeles Times* Syndicate of March 23, 1969, "The Coming Economic Collapse," which predicted that the United States would be forced off the gold standard— an event that actually took place on Aug. 15, 1971; and (5) an article in *The Freeman*, August, 1971, entitled "World Inflation Factory," calling attention once more to "the inherent unsoundness of the International Monetary Fund system."

All of these pieces and their predictions show that the monetary chaos and world inflation could have been stopped, or at least greatly diminished, in 1971, in 1969, in 1949, or even in 1944, if those in positions of power had really understood what they were doing and had combined that understanding with even a minimum of political courage and responsibility.

I wish to express my thanks here to *The New York Times*, *The American Scholar*, The Foundation for Economic Education, *Newsweek*, *The Los Angeles Times* Syndicate, and *The Freeman* for giving me permission to republish these articles.

In my editorials for *The New York Times*, the understatement of the case against the defects of the Bretton Woods agreements was deliberate, because I had always to bear in mind that I was writing not in my own name but that of the newspaper. For one example: in the effort not to seem "extreme", I looked for mitigating merits, and was far too kind to the proposed International Bank, simply because, unlike the Fund, it was not called upon to make enormous loans automatically, but allowed to exercise some discretion. The article setting it up even went so far as to stipulate that a committee selected by the Bank must learn whether a would-be borrower was "in a position to meet its obligations!"

Yet obvious as these dangers should have been, even in 1944, to those who bothered to read the text of the Bretton Woods agreements, I found myself almost alone, particularly in the journalistic world, in calling attention to them. (My editorials mentioned at the time the few persons and groups who did.)

Even today, nearly forty years later, and twelve years after the agreements collapsed from their inherent infirmities, we hear journalistic pleas for their restoration. Even the usually perceptive *Wall Street Journal* published an editorial as late as June 22, 1982, entitled "Bring Back Bretton Woods." It may be said in extenuation that the editorial writer was comparing the situation in 1982, when inconvertible paper currencies were daily depreciating nearly everywhere, with the comparatively stable exchange rates for the 25 years before Bretton Woods openly collapsed in August, 1971, when President Nixon closed the American gold window. But *The Wall Street Journal* forgot that Bretton Woods worked as intended as long as it did only by putting an excessive burden and responsibility on one nation and one currency.

Another and perhaps more typical example of the confusion on this subject that still prevails in the journalistic world today, appeared in a column by Flora Lewis in *The New York Times* of October 19, 1982, entitled "A World Reserve Plan." She began by praising the original Bretton Woods scheme as "a way of admitting that nobody could go it alone and prosper any longer." She then offered a complicated misexplanation of what had gone wrong since then, and ended by suggesting that the real trouble was that President Reagan was preventing the International Monetary Fund from lending even more billions to already bankrupt debtors .

Let us, at the cost of repetition, remind ourselves of what really went wrong. The Bretton Woods agreements never seriously considered the return of each signatory nation to a gold standard. Lord Keynes, their principal author, even boasted that they set up "the exact opposite of a gold standard." In any case, what Bretton Woods really set up was what used to be called a "gold-exchange" standard. Every other country in the scheme undertook simply to keep its own currency unit convertible into dollars. The United States alone undertook (on the demand of foreign central banks) to keep its own currency unit directly convertible into gold.

Neither the politicians of foreign countries, nor unfortunately of our own, realized the awesome responsibility that this scheme put on the American banking and currency authorities to refrain from excessive credit expansion. The result was that when President Nixon closed the American gold window on August 15, 1971, our gold reserves amounted to only about 2 per cent of our outstanding currency and demand and time bank deposits ($10,132 million of gold vs. $454,500 million of M2). In other words, there was only $2.23 in gold to redeem every $100 of paper promises. But this takes no account of outstanding "Eurodollars," or even of the outstanding currency and bank deposits of all the foreign signatories to Bretton Woods. The ultimate gold reserves on which the conversion burden could legally fall under the system must have been only some small fraction of 1 per cent of the total paper obligations against them. Even if the American Congress, and our own banking and currency authorities, had acted far more responsibly, the original Bretton Woods system was inherently impossible to maintain.

A gold-exchange standard can be workable if only a few small countries resort to it. It cannot indefinitely operate when nearly all other countries try to depend on just one for ultimate gold convertibility.

The Bretton Woods system continues to do great harm because the dollar, though no longer based on gold and itself depreciating, continues to be used (as of this writing) as the world's primary reserve currency, while the institutions it set up, like the International Money Fund and the Bank, continue to make immense new loans to irresponsible and improvident governments.

Let us now look chronologically at the world monetary developments of the last forty years. The representatives of some forty-five nations conferred at Bretton Woods from July 1 to July 22, 1944, and drafted Articles of Agreement. It was not until December, 1945, that the required number of countries had ratified the agreements; and not until March 1, 1947, that the International Monetary Fund (IMF), the chief institution set up by the agreements, began financial operations at its headquarters in Washington, D. C.

The ostensible purpose of the IMF was "to promote international monetary cooperation." The chief way it was proposed to do this was to have all the member nations make a quota of their currencies available to be loaned to those member countries "in temporary balance of payment difficulties." The individual nations whose currencies were to be made available were not themselves to decide how large their loans to the borrowing nations should be, nor the period for which the loans were to be made.

This decision was and is, in fact, made by the international bureaucrats who operate the IMF. How these officials decide that these balance of payment problems are merely "temporary" I do not know. In any case, the "temporary" loans normally have run from one to three years. Until recently, the loans were made almost automatically, at the request of the borrowing nation.

It should be obvious on its face that this whole procedure is unsound. It is possible, of course, that a nation could get into balance-of-payments difficulties through no real fault of its own—because of an earthquake, a long drought, or being forced into an essentially defensive war. But most of the time, balance-of-payments difficulties are brought about by unsound policies on the part of the nation that suffers from them. These may consist of pegging its currency too high, encouraging its citizens or its own government to buy excessive imports; encouraging its unions to fix domestic wage rates too high; enacting minimum wage rates; imposing excessive corporation or individual income taxes (destroying incentives to production and preventing the creation of sufficient capital for investment); imposing price ceilings; undermining property rights; attempting to redistribute income; following other anti-capitalistic policies; or even imposing outright socialism. Since nearly every government today—particularly of "developing" countries—is practicing at least a few of these policies, it is not surprising that some of these countries will get into "balance-of-payment difficulties" with others.

A "balance-of-payments difficulty", in short, is most often merely a symptom of a much wider and more basic ailment. If nations with "balance-of-payments" problems did not have a quasi-charitable world government institution to fall back on and were obliged to resort to prudently managed private banks, domestic or foreign, to bail them out, they would be forced to make drastic reforms in their policies to obtain such loans. As it is, the IMF, in effect, encourages them to continue their socialist and inflationist course. The IMF loans not only encourage continued inflation in the borrowing countries, but themselves directly add to world inflation. (These loans, incidentally, are largely made at below-market interest rates.)

But the Fund has increased world inflation in still another way, not contemplated in the original Articles of Agreement of 1944. In 1970, it created a new currency, called "Special Drawing Rights" (SDRs). These SDRs were created out of thin air, by a stroke of the pen. They were created, according to the Fund, "to meet a widespread concern that the growth of international liquidity might be inadequate" (A Keynesian euphemism for not enough paper money).

> These SDRs, in the words of the IMF, were allocated to members—at their option—in proportion to their quotas over specified periods. During the first period, 1970-72, SDR 9.3 billion was allocated. There were no further allocations until January 1, 1979. Amounts of SDR 4 billion each were allocated on January 1, 1979, on January 1, 1980, and January 1, 1981. SDRs in existence now [April, 1982] total SDR 21.4 billion, about 5 per cent of present international non-gold reserves.

In view of the ease with which this fiat world money was created, its limited volume (even though in excess of SDRs 20 billion) may strike many people as surprisingly moderate. But its creation, as we shall see, set an ominous precedent.

I should define more specifically just what an SDR is. From July, 1974, through December, 1980, the SDR was valued on the basis of the market exchange rate for a basket of the currencies of the 16 members with the largest exports of goods and services. Since January, 1981, the basket has been composed of the currencies of the five members with the largest exports of goods and services. The currencies and their weights in the basket are the U. S. dollar (42 per cent), the deutsche mark (19 per cent), and the yen, French franc, and pound sterling (13 per cent each).

The SDR serves as the official unit of account in keeping the books of the IMF. It is designed, in the words of the Fund, to "eventually become the principal asset of the international monetary system."

But it is worth noting a few things about it. Its value changes every day in relation to the dollar and every other national currency. (For example, on August 25, 1982, the SDR was valued at $1.099 and six days later at $1.083.) More importantly, the SDR, composed of a basket of paper currencies, is itself a paper unit governed by a weighted average of inflation in five countries and steadily depreciating in purchasing power.

A number of countries have pegged their currencies to the SDR—i.e., to a falling peg. Yet the IMF boasts that it is still its policy "to reduce gradually the monetary role of gold," and proudly points out that from 1975 to 1980 it sold 50 million ounces of gold—a third of its 1975 holdings. The U.S. Treasury Department can make a similar boast. What neither the Fund nor the American Treasury bother to point out is that this gold has an enormously higher value today than at the time the sales were made. The profit has gone to world speculators and other private persons. The American and, in part, the foreign taxpayer has lost again.

To resume the history of the Bretton Woods agreements and the IMF: Because the Fund was created on completely mistaken assumptions regarding what was wrong and what was needed, its loans went wrong from the very beginning. It began operations on March 1, 1947. In a book published that year, *Will Dollars Save the World**, I was already pointing out (pp. 81-82) that:

> The [International Monetary] Fund in its present form ought not to exist at all. Its managers are virtually without power to insist on internal fiscal and economic reforms before they grant their credits. A $25 million credit granted by the fund to France, for example, is being used to keep the franc far above its real purchasing power and at a level that encourages imports and discourages exports. This merely prolongs the unbalance of French trade and creates a need for still more loans. Such a use of the resources of the Fund not only fails to do any good, but does positive harm.

This loan and its consequences were typical. Yet on Dec. 18, 1946, the IMF contended that the trade deficits of European countries "would not be appreciably narrowed by changes in their currency parities."

The countries themselves finally decided otherwise. On Sept. 18, 1949, precisely to restore its trade balance and "to earn the dollars we need," the government of Great Britain slashed the par value of the pound overnight from $4.03 to $2.80. Within a single week twenty-five nations followed its example

*The Foundation for Economic Education, Irvington-on-Hudson, New York. A 6500 word condensation of it was also published in the January, 1948 issue of *The Reader's Digest* and in all its foreign issues of that month.

was largely the existence of the IMF and its misguided lending that had encouraged a continuance of pernicious economic policies on the part of individual nations—and still does.

Let us now take another jump forward in our history. In a column published on March 23, 1969, "The Coming Monetary Collapse", I predicted that: "The international monetary system set up at Bretton Woods in 1944 is on the verge of breaking down," and "one of these days the United States will be openly forced to refuse to pay out any more of its gold at $35 an ounce even to foreign central banks." This actually occurred two-and-a-half years later, on Aug. 15, 1971.

The fulfillment of this prophecy did not mean that I was the seventh son of a seventh son. I simply pointed in detail to the conditions already existing in March, 1969, that made this outcome inevitable. But next to no one in authority was paying or calling any attention to these conditions—no one except a negligible few.

Since the United States went off gold, and some of the results have become evident, most of the blame for that action (on the part of those who already believed in the gold standard or have since become converted to it) has been put on President Nixon, who made the announcement. He doubtless deserves some of that blame. But the major culprits are those who set up the Bretton Woods system and those who so uncritically accepted it. No single nation's currency could long be expected to hold up the value of all the currencies of the world. Even if the United States had itself pursued a far less inflationary policy in the twenty-seven years from 1944 to 1971, it could not be expected indefinitely to subsidize, through the IMF, had itself pursued a far less inflationary policy in the twenty-seven years from 1944 to 1971, it could not be expected indefinitely to subsidize, through the IMF, the International Bank, and gold conversion, the inflations of other countries. The world dollar-exchange system was inherently brittle, and it broke.

So today we have depreciating inconvertible paper currencies all over the world, an unprecedented situation that has already caused appalling anxiety and human misery. Yet the supreme irony is that the Bretton Woods institutions that have failed so completely in their announced purpose, and led to only monetary chaos instead, are still there, still operating, still draining the countries with lower inflations to subsidize the higher inflations of others.

Yet to describe exactly what the IMF has done up to the present moment is not easy to do in non-technical terms. The Fund has its own jargon. Its books are kept in Special Drawing Rights (SDRs) which are artificial entries and nobody's pocket money. Its loans are seldom called loans but "purchases," because a country uses its own money unit to "buy," through the IMF, SDRs, dollars, or any other national currencies. Repayments to the Fund are called "repurchases of purchases."

So, as of Sept. 30, 1982, total purchases, including "reserve tranche" purchases, on the IMF's books since it began operations have amounted to SDR 66,567 million (U.S. $71,879 million). Again, as of Sept. 30, 1982, total repurchases of purchases amounted to SDR 36,744 million.

The total amount of loans outstanding as of Sept. 30, 1982, was SDR 16,697 million (U.S. $18,020 million). The leading half-dozen borrowers were: India, SDR 1,766 million; Yugoslavia, SDR 1,469 million; Turkey, SDR 1,346 million; South Korea, SDR 1,148 million; Pakistan, SDR 1,079 million; and the Philippines, SDR 780 million—a total of SDR 7,588 million or $8,193 million in U.S. currency.

The future, of course, can only be guessed at, but the outlook is ominous. A sobering glance ahead was published in *The New York Times* of Jan. 9, 1983. The IMF's total outstanding loans had then risen to $21 billion. The executive directors of the Fund had just approved a $3.9 billion loan designed as an emergency bailout of the near bankrupt Mexico. The Fund had also agreed to a similar package for Argentina. One for Brazil had been almost completed. Lined up for further help from the Fund, which already had loans out to thirty-three hard-pressed countries, were Chile, the Philippines, and Portugal.

Many had feared in the fall of 1982 that Mexico would simply refuse to make payments on its $85 billion foreign debt, thereby creating an even worse international financial crisis. So the Managing Director of the IMF, the Frenchman Jacques de Larosière, before making the loan, warned the private banks that had already lent billions to Mexico that unless they came up with more, they might find themselves with nothing at all. He met a delegation representing 1,400 commercial banks with loans out to Mexico. Before one additional cent would be put up by the IMF, he told them, the private banks would have to roll over $20 billion of their credits to Mexico maturing between August, 1982, and the end of 1984, and extend $5 billion in fresh loans. Similar conditions were later attached to the Fund's loans to Argentina and Brazil.

So the IMF is now using its loans as leverage to force the extension of old and the making of new private loans.   All this may seem momentarily reassuring. At least it tries to put the main part of the future burden and risk on the imprudent past private lenders (and their creditors in turn) rather than on the world's taxpayers and national currency holders.

But what is all this leading to? May it not consist merely of throwing good money after bad? How long can the international jugglers keep the mounting unpaid debt in the air?

They cannot be blamed for not making a new try. On Jan. 17, 1983, senior monetary officials from 10 major industrial nations (the Group of 10, formed in 1962) agreed to make available a $20 billion emergency fund to help deeply indebted countries. As reported in *The New York Times* of Jan. 18, 1983:

> The new fund is to be established by tripling the Group of 10's current commitment to lend the IMF an additional $7 billion whenever it runs short of money and by relaxing the rules under which this aid is provided. ... Major industrial governments also plan to increase the IMF's own lendable capital this year by about 50 per cent, to $90 billion. The government authorities hope that private banks then would also help these countries by agreeing to delay debt payments and providing more credit so the poorer countries would not be forced to curb imports and thus deepen the world recession.

Thus, the rescuing governments plan to throw still more money at near-bankrupt countries to encourage them to continue the very policies of over-spending that brought on their predicament.

In an editorial on January 25, 1983, *The Wall Street Journal* commented: "What started out as a relatively modest effort to increase international monetary reserves is turning into an all-out assault on the U.S. Treasury—led by the Secretary of the Treasury himself."

The prospect is made even more disturbing when one looks about in vain among the world's statesmen or putative financial leaders for anyone with a clear proposal for bringing the increasing expansion of credit to an end. The present American Secretary of the Treasury, Donald T. Regan, for example, is reported to be "worried that too much IMF induced austerity could bring about even sharper contractions in world economic activity".

And among the influential politicians in office today he is not alone, but typical. In 1971, when President Nixon was imposing wage and price controls, he said: "We are all Keynesians now." He was not far wrong. Even politicians who do not consider themselves inflationists are afraid to advocate bringing inflation to a halt. They merely recommend slowing down the rate. But doing this would at best prolong and increase depression where it already exists and prolong and increase the consequent unemployment. It would be like trying to reduce a man's pain by cutting off his gangrenous leg a little bit at a time.

In order for inflation, once begun, to continue having any stimulative effect, its pace must be constantly accelerated. Prices and purchases must turn out to be higher than expected. The only course for a government that has begun inflating, if it hopes to avoid hyper-inflation and a final "crack-up boom", is to stop inflating completely, to balance its budget without delay, and to make sure its citizens understand that this is what it is doing.

22

This would, of course, bring a crisis, but much less net damage than a policy of gradualism. As the Nobel laureate F. A. Hayek said recently* in recommending a similar course: "The choices are 20 per cent unemployment for six months or 10 per cent unemployment for three years." I cannot vouch for his exact percentage and time-span guesses, but they illustrate the kind of alternative involved in the choice.

To resume our history: On Feb. 12, 1983, the IMF approved an increase in its lending resources of 47.4 per cent to a total of $98.9 billion, the largest increase proposed in its history.

Some commentators began pointing out that the IMF was already holding gold at a market value of between $40 and $50 billion, second only to the holdings of the U.S. government, and suggested it might start selling off some of this gold to raise the money to make its intended new loans.

On April 4, William E. Simon, the former U.S. Secretary of the Treasury, now free to express his personal opinion frankly, wrote in an article in *The Wall Street Journal*:

> We are witnessing the tragic spectacle of the deficit-ridden rescuing the bankrupt with an outpouring of more American red ink—and the taxpayer is left holding the bag....By extending credit to countries beyond their ability to repay, the final bankruptcy is worse....There is no point to a bailout that increases world debt when the problem is too much indebtedness already. Countries are in trouble because they cannot service their current obligations. The strain on

*Interview in *Silver and Gold Report*, end of December, 1982. (P.O.Box 325, Newtown, Conn. 06470)

them is not eased by a bailout that loads them up with more.

I may add my own comment that government-to-government loans made through an international pool reverse all normal incentives. These loans go mainly to the countries that have got themselves into trouble by following wasteful and anti-capitalistic policies—policies which the loans themselves then encourage and enable them to continue.

When governments are obliged to turn to private lenders, the latter will usually insist on policies by the borrowing governments that will enable the loans to be repaid. There has recently been an outbreak of justifiable criticism of private banks for making improvident loans to Third World countries. What has been until very recently overlooked is that it is precisely because these private banks have been counting on the IMF to bail them out in case of default that a great part of these dubious loans were made.''

On May 9, 1983, President Mitterrand of France called for a conference "at the highest level" to reorganize the world monetary system. "The time has really come," he said, "to think in terms of a new Bretton Woods." He forgot that it was precisely because under the old Bretton Woods system American gold reserves were drawn upon and wasted, among other things to keep the paper franc far above its market level, that the system broke down. Only a return to a genuine international gold standard (and not a pretence of one accompanied by a multitude of national inflations) can bring lasting world currency stability.

On June 8 the Senate approved the bill to increase the IMF's lending resources by a total of $43 billion,

24

with an increase of $8.4 billion in the contribution of the U.S. On August 3 the House passed a similar bill, with more restrictive amendments. But Congressmen Ron Paul of Texas declared: "The total U.S. commitment in H.R. 2957 is about $25 billion, not merely the $8.4 billion for the IMF, as one might be led to believe by the press."

But even before the bill was passed, some international bankers were predicting that the additional appropriation would not be enough. On Nov. 18, 1983, in the last day of its session, Congress finally passed a compromise bill, along with a slue of other legislation, increasing the American contribution to the IMF by $8.4 million. But it attached an irrelevant rider authorizing $15.6 billion for subsidized housing programs, so that the President would be forced to approve this expenditure also.

Let us take a look at the international debt situation as it stands at the moment of writing this. The demand for increased lending by the IMF and other institutions arose in the fall of 1982 because of the huge debts of Mexico, Argentina and other Latin American countries. In the twelve months following, commercial banks around the world renegotiated repayment terms for $90 billion worth of debt owed by fifteen countries. This was twenty times more than the amount restructured in any previous year, according to a study by the Group of Thirty, an international economic research body. Yet on Sept. 5, 1983, *The New York Times* published the following table:

Latin America's Debt

In billions of dollars

	Total Debt	Debt Owed U.S. Banks
Argentina	$36.5	$8.6
Brazil	86.3	22.0
Chile	17.2	5.9
Colombia	10.5	3.7
Ecuador	6.7	2.1
Mexico	84.6	24.3
Peru	11.6	2.4
Venezuela	32.6	11.2

Source: Morgan Guaranty Trust Company

The world cannot get back to economic sanity until the IHF is abolished. So long as it stands ready to make more bad loans, near-bankrupt countries will continue to go into further debt.

The Bretton Woods agreements, drafted in 1944, and the International Monetary Fund set up by them, were not the sole causes of the present world inflation. But they constituted a major contribution. They were built on the assumption that inflation—the continuous expansion of international paper credit, and the continuous making of loans by an international governmental institution—were the proper and necessary ways to "promote world economic growth." This assumption was disastrously false. We will not stop the growth of world inflation and world socialism until the institutions and policies adopted to promote them have been abolished.

Part I

Birth of the Bretton Woods System

Hopes had been raised ten years earlier, but the Bretton Woods agreement never seriously considered the return of each signatory nation to the gold standard.

1

The Return to Gold

July 9, 1934

The presence at Basle of Governor Harrison of the New York Federal Reserve Bank is a favorable sign, particularly when we learn that he has been conferring there with Governor Norman of the Bank of England. Whether the two have been discussing the stabilization of the pound and the dollar, or the eventual return of both to a fixed gold standard, will probably remain for the present in the realm of conjecture. The knowledge that that problem was at last being dealt with, however, would be extremely heartening. We can hardly expect a vigorous and continued world recovery so long as the two principal world currencies remain subject to fluctuation and uncertainty.

The view is sometimes expressed that the United States has already returned to the gold standard. It is a very equivocal gold currency, however, that can be changed in value overnight by nearly 15 per cent at the decision of one man. Our Government could return to a genuine fixed gold standard acting alone. But announcement of such a plan would not have half the immediate buoyant effect on world confidence that a joint announcement by the two great

31

English speaking countries would have. The latter would not only restore stability to the two major units of value, but would symbolize a return to international collaboration in a world that has been drifting steadily toward a more and more intense nationalism.

One cause for hope of an early agreement is that many of the illusions concerning the advantage of drifting currencies and competitive depreciation have been dissolving under the test of experience. Great increases in export trade have not followed depreciation; the usual result of anchorless currencies has been a shrinkage of both export and import trade. Again, the fallacy is beginning to be apparent of the idea that a currency allowed to drift would finally "seek its own natural level." It is becoming clear that the "natural" level of a currency is precisely what governmental policies in the long run tend to make it. There is no more a "natural value" for an irredeemable currency than there is for a promissory note of a person of uncertain intentions to pay an undisclosed sum at an unspecified date. Finally, it has been learned that competitive depreciation, unlike competitive armaments, is a game that no Government is too poor or too weak to play, and that it can lead to nothing but general demoralization.

Instead of putting its emphasis on the need for each country to keep its own currency strong by maintaining convertibility, by keeping its budget in balance, and by refraining from inflation, trade barriers, and exchange restrictions, the Bretton Woods agreement proposed that the strong currencies should subsidize the weak. It lost sight of the fact that the chief duty of the United States was to maintain the integrity of the dollar.

2

For Stable Exchanges
June 1, 1944

The United Nations Monetary and Financial Conference called by the President will meet a month from today. Its purpose is the highly desirable one of securing stable exchange rates in the post-war world. But the recent proposal for an $8,000,000,000 International Stabilization Fund misconceives the nature of the problem and approaches it from the wrong end. Essentially it seeks to fix the value of each nation's currency unit in relation to the others by arranging to have the fund buy the weak currencies and to sell the strong currencies at the parities fixed. It is obvious that a weak currency will drop to its true market value as soon as such purchases cease. As long, however, as the purchases continue, the nations with strong currencies will be subsidizing the nations with weak currencies (or at least the private holders of those currencies), and thereby subsidizing also the internal economic policies, whatever they may happen to be, of the nations with weak currencies. The United States, as the chief contributor to the fund, would be the chief loser; but the money that it poured out in this way might not only fail to help world recovery but, by prolonging unsound policies within the nations whose currencies could only be held up by such purchases, might actually do harm.

The true solution of this problem would begin at the other end. It would seek to make currencies sound within each country. If each nation can maintain the integrity of its own currency, if each nation keeps its own monetary unit at par, then the problem of maintaining a stable relationship between different currencies will solve itself. The true object of the forthcoming monetary conference, therefore, should be to lay down the principles and explore the methods by which this can be done.

The broad principles should not be difficult to formulate. One requirement for a stable currency is that it be redeemable in something that is itself fixed and definite: for all practical purposes this means a return to the historic gold standard. Another requirement for a stable currency is a balanced budget. A third requirement is that Governments refrain from currency and credit inflation. A fourth is a removal of, or at least a great reduction in, the pre-war barriers to international trade—tariffs, quotas, exchange restrictions, and all the rest.

These requirements form a unit. If one of them is violated it will be difficult, if not impossible, to fulfill the others. Thus if a nation's budget is chronically unbalanced it is practically compelled to resort to borrowing through currency or credit inflation to make up the difference. When it does this it undermines faith in its currency unit and cannot maintain gold payments. Officials of the Government then say that the gold standard "has broken down," when they really mean that their own policies have broken it.

There will be grave problems after the war for almost every nation fixing a new currency parity at a level where it can be held. But the belief that only a rich nation can afford a gold standard is a fallacy. As Viscount Goschen, one of England's ablest Chancellors of the Exchequer, once said: "Our powers of obtaining gold would only be exhausted when the country had nothing left to sell."

The greatest single contribution the United States could make to world currency stability after the war is to announce its determination to stabilize its own currency. It will incidentally help us, of course, if other nations as well return to the gold standard. They will do it, however, only to the extent that they recognize that they are doing it not primarily as a favor to us but to themselves.

*The agreement provided in advance for a **uniform** devaluation in the gold value of member currencies. This deliberately sanctioned future world inflation.*

3

For World Inflation?

June 24, 1944

In the statement of principles for the proposed International Stabilization Fund is this short paragraph:

> An agreed uniform change may be made in the gold value of member currencies provided every member country having 10 per cent or more of the aggregate quotas approves.

This is a provision which would permit world inflation. Experience has shown that it is extremely unlikely that any Government will wish to raise the unit gold value of its currency, thereby bringing about an internal drop in prices or wages. The political pressures from time immemorial, and particularly in the last three decades, have been in the direction of devaluation and inflation. There are few countries in which the most vociferous pressure groups are not in favor, at almost any time, of devaluation or inflation that would raise farm prices or wage rates, or remove unemployment caused by wage rates too high in relation to the existing price level, or to relieve debtors, particularly the Government itself, which will be urged to write down the burden of its internal debt by the device of inflation.

A provision for *uniform* inflation in all major countries would increase the temptation to inflate in each country by removing some immediate penalties. When the currency of a single country begins to sag because of inflationary policies, two embarrassing results follow. One is the immediate loss of gold, unless the Government prohibits its export (which makes the currency sag more); the other is the humiliation of seeing the country's currency quoted at a discount in other nations. A uniform inflation in the world's most important countries would avoid both of these embarrassments.

But the real evils of inflation would remain. Persons with fixed salaries or wages would see their purchasing power shrink. Pensioners would see the purchasing power of their pensions shrink. Holders of Government bonds, often bought for purely patriotic reasons, would see the purchasing power of their capital and interest shrink. Capital in the form of bonds or mortgages would be much harder to borrow; and, therefore, many buildings would not be erected and many enterprises would not be started, because of the prospect of this inflation.

It would be difficult to think of a more serious threat to world stability and full production than the continual prospect of a uniform world inflation to which the politicians of every country would be so easily tempted.

The agreement provided that any country could reduce the par value of its currency whenever this was necessary to correct a "fundamental disequilibrium", and that the proposed International Monetary Fund should not reject such a proposal. "Fundamental disequilibrium" was not defined. No limit was put on the number of these reductions of parity provided they were individually 10 per cent or less. After having had its currency accepted at par by other members, any member country could withdraw from the Fund at any time, provided it gave notice in writing. No time period was specified for how long in advance such notice was required.

4

How Will It Stabilize?

June 26, 1944

One of the ostensible objects of the proposed International Stabilization Fund is "to promote exchange stability." The more the "statement of principles" for the fund is examined, however, the more difficult it becomes to find exchange stability in it. It provides, indeed, that when any nation enters the fund a par value for its currency shall be fixed or stated; but this can apparently be changed at any time. A member country may propose a change in the par value of its currency, for example, if it considers such a change "appropriate to the correction of a fundamental disequilibrium." A "fundamental disequilibrium" is not defined in the statement. No country that wishes to devaluate should find great difficulty in arguing that it wishes to do so to correct a "fundamental disequilibrium."

The statement of principles continues:

The fund shall approve a requested change in the par value of a member's currency if it is essential to the correction of a fundamental disequilibrium. In particular the fund shall not reject a requested change, necessary to restore

43

equilibrium, because of the domestic, social or political policies of the country applying for a change.

In other words, the nations which have been supporting that country's currency cannot reject a devaluation merely because the "fundamental disequilibrium" complained of has been the direct result of unsound internal policies.

The statement of principles provides that a member country may reduce the established parity of its currency by 10 per cent. "In the case of application for a further change, not covered by the above and not exceeding 10 per cent, the fund shall give its decision within two days of receiving the application, if the applicant so requests." This is a little ambiguous but seems to imply that a nation can devalue a further 10 per cent with the consent of the fund. Suppose the nation wishes to devaluate still further? This seems to be provided for under Section VIII, Paragraph 1: "A member country may withdraw from the fund by giving notice in writing." The length of the notice is not specified: apparently the member country's withdrawal could take place immediately after the notice was received.

In other words, while under the plan the net creditor nations pledge themselves through their contributions to the fund to buy each net debtor member nation's currency to keep it at parity, they have no assurance that the value of these currency holdings will not suddenly shrink through a sudden act of devaluation on the part of the nations whose currencies they hold.

The guiding idea of the conference, even at its opening, was that the value of the weak currencies should be maintained by the countries with strong currencies agreeing to buy them at a fixed rate, regardless of their market value. This could only weaken the strong currencies. The one real cure was disregarded: to encourage each country to refrain from inflation and to maintain the integrity of its own monetary unit.

5

The Monetary Conference

July 1, 1944

Today the representatives of more than forty nations will gather at Bretton Woods to open a monetary conference. In several respects the conference will get off to an unfortunate start. Important as the problem of stable exchanges and world monetary soundness is, it would be impossible to imagine a more difficult time for individual nations to decide at what level they can fix and stabilize their national currency unit. How could the representatives of France, of Holland, of Greece, of China, make any but the wildest guess at this moment of the point at which they could hope to stabilize? This problem exists on a world-wide scale to a greater extent than ever before in history.

It is perhaps an even more serious obstacle to success that the main proposal for stabilization the conference is scheduled to consider quite misconceives the nature of the problem to be solved and therefore attempts to solve it from the wrong end. It proposes that each nation shall adopt a par value for its currency that the other nations shall accept; that the nations shall put gold or their own paper currencies into a common pool, and that the resources of that pool

47

shall be used to try to keep each currency at par by a commitment to buy the weak currencies with the strong currencies. The fund is not to exercise any real control, however, over the internal policies of the countries with the weak currencies.

It is obvious that such a plan could maintain even the outward appearance of success only for a short time. It is possible, of course, to keep a valueless currency at any arbitrarily chosen level by a commitment to pay that price for it, just as it is possible to keep a worthless stock at $100 a share by buying at that price all of the stock that is offered for sale. But when the allotted resources of the buyer run out, the currency or the stock will immediately drop to its natural level, and the buyer will find himself holding just that much worthless paper. The plan becomes particularly unrealistic when each nation can turn out unlimited amounts of its own currency on its own printing presses—with the incentive, which it does not ordinarily have, of a buyer at a fixed price. It seems probable that the plan could only lead to a huge waste of funds and to a temporary world inflation with a subsequent collapse.

On the positive side, what could and should be done at the Bretton Woods conference? Much would be gained by an agreement on certain fundamental principles. The first essential is a determination to make currencies sound within each country. The United States is in a position to take the leadership. The most important contribution that this country could make to world currency stability would be to declare unequivocally its determination to stabilize its own currency. It could do this by announcing its determination to balance its budget at the earliest practicable moment after the war, and by announcing that the dollar would no longer be on a "twenty-four" hour basis, and subject to every rumor, but firmly anchored to a fixed quantity of gold. This nation would also have to make clear that it was willing to take the initiative in lowering its own tariff barriers, whether or not other nations were willing to follow, and that we for our part would refrain from import quotas and exchange restrictions. Even if we adopted such a program only partially it would be of immense help. We could then urge other countries to follow our example, not for our benefit, but for their own.

It is true that the present fashionable fiscal theories stand in the way of such primary reforms. But the United States will hold one great inducement for securing them. Most other countries will need help in returning to a sound currency and sound internal policies. We are in a position to supply it. We can offer moderate gold loans in return for such reforms. The reforms would not only be in the direct interest of the nations making them, but not unless they were made would our loans have a reasonable prospect of repayment.

So far as possible, the loans should be made by American private investors, who, through their representatives, would be in a much better position diplomatically to insist on sound policies within the borrowing nation than our own Government would be. But for a limited period of years, and solely for stabilization loans, there may be an advantage in having Government participation, either on some such basis as that of FHA mortgages or by the Government taking 5 or 10 per cent of individual loans. Government participation of this sort might increase both the volume of such loans and the promptness with which they were placed, at the same time as the dominant private interest would take the loans out of the dangerous political field and assure that they were made on business principles and with adequate guarantees.

But any machinery that is set up will be of secondary importance for world recovery compared with ideological reforms. Each nation should abandon the fallacious idea that it is to its own advantage to inflate or devaluate, or that it gains when it erects huge tariff barriers or subsidizes exports or blocks its currency, or when it forbids its own citizens to export gold, capital, or credit. Each nation should abandon the fallacious idea, in short, that it gains when it makes economic war on its neighbor.

Nearly every nation represented at Bretton Woods sought to increase its "quota" in the Fund, because this meant not what each one would have to put into the Fund but what it hoped to draw out. On the basis of this quota it could "buy" currencies of real value—meaning, in the main, American dollars—to twice the amount of its quota. This could encourage inflation in such countries and prove very expensive—and wasteful— for the United States.

6

Results at Bretton Woods

July 18, 1944

Genuine international economic cooperation after the war will be possible only if there is a profound change from the ideology of the Thirties. Nations must learn that their own economic salvation is not to be attained by making economic war upon their neighbors. They must learn that prohibitive tariffs, import quotas, competitive depreciation, exchange controls, blocked currencies, restrictions on capital export, are the road to economic disaster. The return of international peace and prosperity will be possible only if these devices are abandoned and if the neo-mercantilist fallacies that give rise to them are abandoned also. To achieve this international cooperation will require not only generosity and goodwill on our par but, above all, clarity of thought.

The Administration has shown the good-will and the generosity. These have reflected themselves in such an indispensable institution as UNRRA [United Nations Relief and Rehabilitation Administration]. Unfortunately, in the proposals that the Administration has sponsored at Bretton Woods it has failed to show clarity of thought. The result is a plan confused in its objectives and hazardous in its possibilities.

The delegates at Bretton Woods—above all, the American delegates—seem to be obsessed by the idea of machinery. They act as if international economic cooperation could be achieved only by setting up some elaborate organization, with funds and quotas and votes and rules and whereases, and as if the mere existence of such machinery in itself constituted a solution of the problem. In their determined efforts to secure agreement on the superficial problems of machinery they have failed to secure or even to seek agreement on the really basic problem of principles.

The key to the kind of organization they have been setting up can be found in the struggle of nearly every nation to increase its "quota" in the fund. For this "quota", apart from that of the United States, represents fundamentally not what each nation puts into the fund but what it hopes to take out of it.. The real assets of the fund will consist of its gold and of whatever currencies are reliably convertible into gold or even into wanted goods. But each country will make a maximum contribution in gold of only 25 per cent of its quota, and in many cases the percentage contribution in gold will be far below that. For the rest it can throw in its own paper money, valued at an arbitrary figure, whether or not it is convertible into gold or represents anything but the product of the printing press. On the basis of this quota it can "buy" currencies of real value—meaning in the main American dollars—to twice the amount of its quota.

In simpler terms, by putting in a very small quantity in gold, a country can borrow many times that amount in dollars or other valuable currencies. In still simpler terms, this means that America agrees in advance to lend each of more than forty other countries up to a certain fixed amount of dollars, whether or not there is any reasonable prospect of repayment, and regardless of the internal economic policies of each country or what it does with the money. This not only means that we can lose many dollars in bad loans, but, what is more important, that as long as credit is available to nations under these easy conditions they will postpone unpleasant but essential economic reforms.

What is needed above all is an agreement on sound principles. Through UNRRA we should give to the former occupied countries promptly and generously whatever is needed to relieve hunger and distress. Humanitarian gifts, however, should not be confused with business loans. No loan should be automatic in amount or made without conditions. It should be granted only where there is real prospect of repayment, and only on consideration of the adoption of sound internal economic policies in each borrowing country. America, as the strongest financial country in the world, could not in consistency impose conditions and principles that it was unwilling to adopt first of all for itself. The greatest contribution that America can make to international cooperation is to take the lead in removing excessive barriers against imports, in announcing a determination to halt deficit financing and to balance the budget as soon as possible after the war, and in revealing a determination to stabilize the dollar in terms of a fixed quantity of gold. That policy, in turn, would supply not only an example but an anchor for other currencies.

Because Lord Keynes thought it "worse than a mistake to attempt the invidious task of discriminating between members and assessing their credit worthiness," bad borrowers with bad records and bad internal policies were to get loans from the Fund and the Bank on the same terms as good borrowers with the best records and sound internal policies—thus assuring a further loss and waste of scarce world capital.

7

An International Bank?

July 19, 1944

The drive for a $10,000,000,000 International Bank for Reconstruction and Development illustrates once more the fetish of machinery that possesses the minds of the governmental delegates at Bretton Woods. Like the proposed $8,800,000,000 International Monetary Fund, it rests on the assumption that nothing will be done right unless a grandiose formal intergovernmental institution is set up to do it. It assumes that nothing will be run well unless Governments run it. One institution is to be piled upon another, even though their functions duplicate each other. Thus the proposed Fund is clearly a lending institution, by whatever name it may be called; its purpose is to bolster weak currencies by loans of strong currencies.

One of the difficulties being experienced in the formation of the Bank, however, is the opposite of that found in the formation of the Fund, and serves to illustrate the real nature of the latter. Nations that were fighting for the largest possible quotas in the Fund are fighting for the smallest possible subscriptions to the Bank. That is because the Fund quotas at bottom represented potential borrowing, whereas the Bank subscriptions represent potential lending or losses. It is after the Bank has been set up, and the applications for loans come in, that various nations will again seek the maximum amounts.

Under a free world economy, with private lenders risking their own funds and borrowers seeking to meet their requirements, loans would go to the countries and projects that offered the most attractive terms commensurate with the best prospect of repayment. This means, in general, that capital would go into the countries providing the soundest conditions and into projects promising the greatest economic success. Under such conditions there is the maximum development of world productivity in proportion to the capital invested.

These conditions hardly seem likely to be filled, however, under the proposed international bank plan as envisaged by its framers. Lord Keynes has proposed that the commission to be paid by borrowers should be the same for all members, as it would be "worse than a mistake to attempt the invidious task of discriminating between members and assessing their credit-worthiness." This seems to mean that bad borrowers with bad records and bad internal policies are to pay interest rates no higher than good borrowers with the best records and sound internal policies. When the criterion of credit-worthiness is dismissed as "invidious," moreover, the implication is that loans themselves are to be made without regard to it. Under such conditions the proportion of bad loans and of defaults seems certain to be high, and much capital, in a world already faced by grave shortages, is likely to be dissipated in ill-advised enterprises.

This brings us to the proposed nature of the Bank itself. It would be apparently a bank that "guaranteed" loans made by private investors instead

58

of making loans directly itself. But if this guarantee fully covered both capital and interest, then the private investors making the loan would not have to exercise any care or discrimination on their own account. They would have to conform merely with the requirements of the Bank, which would assume all the losses and risks without having the privilege of directly making the loans. The member Governments acting as directors of the Bank would also be the chief borrowers from the Bank.

Many questions of practical operation also arise. Suppose nation X defaults on its share of the loan. Suppose nation Y then defaults on its share of the guarantee. Who is to guarantee the guarantors? Will the subscriptions to the Bank be in gold, or wholly or mainly in each nation's currency, convertible or inconvertible? Will each nation meet its share of the guarantee merely in its own currency, which may have greatly shrunk in value?

World economic revival will not necessarily flow from a plan under which taxpayers are saddled by their own Governments with losses from huge foreign loans made regardless of their soundness. It is likely, rather, to flow from a situation in which each country, or each industrial venture in it, is encouraged or forced to follow sound policies in order to attract foreign investors.

The Monetary Fund, as set up, I believed would lead to the opposite of its declared purposes. One of those declared purposes, for example, was "to promote exchange stability," but the specific provisions for the Fund not only permitted but encouraged internal inflation, devaluation and exchange instability.

8

The Monetary Fund
July 24, 1944

The final text of the articles of agreement of the proposed International Monetary Fund differs very little,
except in the elaboration of details, from the proposal
submitted before the conference met. In view of the
instructions of the President to the American delegation, this is not surprising. In a letter to Secretary
Morgenthau, the United States delegation chairman,
on June 9, Mr. Roosevelt wrote: "You and the other
delegates will be expected to adhere to the joint statement of principles of an international monetary fund
announced April 21, 1944. You ...are authorized ...to
agree to modifications...provided that such modifications do not fundamentally alter the principles set
forth in the joint statement." These instructions were
unfortunate. They prevented the very discussion of
basic principles that was most essential, and made
the conference, in effect, a rubber stamp which did
little more than endorse the previous work of
the technicians.

The result is that the final agreement meets none of
the fundamental criticisms that applied to the ten-
tative agreement. A vast machinery is provided
which is confused in its objectives. One of the six

declared purposes of the Fund is "to promote exchange stability." But again and again provisions are included to promote instability. The Fund is not allowed to raise any objection if a nation devalues its currency by 10 per cent. It must give an answer within three days if the nation wants to devalue a further 10 per cent. It must concur in practically any proposed devaluation if the change is necessary "to correct a fundamental disequilibrium." It is not allowed to object to a proposed devaluation "because of the domestic, social or political policies of the member proposing" the devaluation. In other words, the Fund cannot criticize internal policies even if they are the direct cause of the devaluation. And the final agreement retains the provisions to authorize a world-wide inflation.

Another declared purpose of the Fund is "the elimination of foreign exchange restrictions." But the detailed proposal itself not only permits but encourages and necessitates foreign exchange restrictions. "The post-war transitional period" is made an exception, during which nations may introduce or continue whatever foreign exchange restrictions they want. The "post-war transitional period" is not precisely defined, but is apparently to last at least three to five years. Even after this any nation may "regulate international capital movements," and in some cases will be even requested to do so. If a currency becomes "scarce," other nations may ration that currency and "impose limitations on the freedom of exchange operations in the scarce currency." All this implies a return to the foreign exchange restrictions developed in the Thirties. It implies a world in which individuals will act under more, not less,

62

government coercion and will have less freedom to buy and sell and make payments where they like.

The proposed agreement sets up a huge machinery and ignores all the basic principles which must be adopted if such machinery could hope to be successful. The American money poured into supporting weak foreign currencies will be worse than wasted, unless the loans are made conditional upon internal reforms in the borrowing nations. Such nations must eschew resort to financing by the printing press. They must prepare to balance their budgets and make their currency convertible into gold or into a gold-convertible currency at par. The United States must take the lead in these reforms. Only on these conditions will genuine currency stability, freedom of world trade, and continuous international cooperation be possible.

What was contemplated in the Bretton Woods agreements and in the 1944 proposed international commodity agreements was not freedom for individuals in different countries to trade with one another on their own terms, but a world in which international prices and trade would be State-dominated. This would only lead to failures, as in the past, and to dangerous international antagonisms.

9

To Make Trade Free

July 27, 1944

The agreements reached at Bretton Woods and the Administration's plans for international talks looking to post-war commodity agreements combine to form a pattern of the kind of post-war economic world that our Government and certainly a number of other Governments have in view. From the standpoint of traditional freedom of trade the outlook is not an encouraging one. When Adam Smith made his great plea for freedom of trade in a world strangled by governmental obstacles and prohibitions, the freedom that he had in mind was that of the individuals directly concerned. "In every country," he wrote, "it always is and must be the interest of the great body of the people to buy whatever they want of those who sell it cheapest." The freedom of the individual buyer corresponded to the freedom of the individual seller, who likewise, Adam Smith argued, should be free to sell in the best market and presumably to take payment in the manner that he himself chose in return. But it is certainly not this kind of freedom, the freedom of the individual citizens of each country, that the Bretton Woods agreements or the proposed commodity agreements have in mind. On the contrary, these agreements presuppose a world in which the type of governmental controls developed in the Twenties and Thirties are to be expanded and systematized. What is contemplated is a world in which international trade is State-dominated.

An interdepartmental committee of technicians is working in Washington on a program for agreements to "stabilize" the price of international commodities. If the experience of the Twenties and Thirties proved anything, one would have thought that it demonstrated above all not only the futility but the harm of this sort of state "stabilization." Even if we assume that we had a body of the ablest and most disinterested economists controlling the system, they would not be able to fix the "right" price for international commodities. They could not know and weigh properly the thousands of factors that go to form such prices and that determine their fluctuations from day to day. But, as a matter of fact, the Government experts are not always experts and they are almost never disinterested. They are usually the servants of pressure groups within their own countries. Almost invariably, as a result of the demands of their own growers or producers, their idea of "stabilizing" a commodity is to price it too high.

Out of scores of examples we need merely recall what happened in the inter-war period in the case of rubber and cotton. The British rubber producers, who had almost a world monopoly, restricted exports to force up the price. The first result was intense resentment in America, the chief consuming country. But the longer result was that the Dutch and other non-British countries expanded their production of rubber so that the scheme ultimately left the British rubber growers in a far worse position than if it had never been put into effect. Similarly, the United States kept up the price of cotton artificially before the war by acreage restriction and Government loans. The result was not only that we lost foreign markets and had to put more than a whole year's supply of cotton in storage, but that we encouraged an increase of cotton growing all over the world, thus permanently injuring American cotton growers.

There is reported to be dissent within the interdepartmental committee of technicians now working on the commodity agreements proposals. Representatives of the Department of Agriculture are represented as desiring permanent instead of merely temporary international commodity agreements, while other experts hold that such agreements fixing prices and production on world markets would be inconsistent with our governmental opposition to cartels. This is perfectly true. And in addition to this inconsistency we must remember that the nations that are the chief consumers of the raw materials will resent the fixing of prices above the natural market and that such economic disagreements will lead to dangerous political antagonisms.

There is a grave danger that the phrase "international cooperation" may be perverted to mean the drawing up of agreements between Governments to control at every point the economic transactions of their own citizens. In the economic field, on the contrary, true international cooperation means the termination of such governmental controls, which are invariably conducted in the interests of political pressure groups, and the return to a world in which men are free to trade and produce at the prices fixed by supply and demand and competitive efficiency.

The plan put forward by Winthrop W. Aldrich, Chairman of the Board of the Chase National Bank, deserved serious study. His objections to the Bretton Woods proposals—that their net effect would be for the good currencies to "be pulled down to the level of the poor currencies"—merited particular attention.

10

Mr. Aldrich's Monetary Plan

September 19, 1944

Winthrop W. Aldrich, Chairman of the Board of the Chase National Bank, suggests as a substitute for the plans advanced at the Bretton Woods conference the negotiation of international agreements for the removal of trade barriers and the establishment of a stable dollar-sterling exchange rate. Whatever may be the final verdict upon the merits of his proposal, his analysis of the proposed International Fund and Bank is thoughtful and impressive, and his own positive proposals make it obvious that his viewpoint is far from that of an economic nationalist.

Mr. Aldrich points out that under the instructions from the President both the American delegation at Bretton Woods and the delegations of other countries were committed to a particular monetary plan in advance and were not free to work anew on the problem or to consider an alternative approach. The powers of the Fund "seem to be obscure and uncertain." Its objectives "lack the focus essential to its success." The United States, by far the largest contributor, will be called upon to supply "about 70 per cent" of the real lendable assets of the Fund. "Inasmuch as the Fund gives nations with relatively poor currencies access, on an automatic basis, to relatively good currencies, the good currencies may be pulled down to the level of the poor currencies." Mr. Aldrich cites the many liberal provisions for alterations in exchange rates, and fears that under them "exchange depreciation would undoubtedly become an accepted and normal procedure in international financial affairs." Proposals for exchange depreciation, indeed, "would be inevitable, since the plan attacks the symptoms rather than the basic causes of exchange instability." The effect of the Fund provisions, he fears also, would be to increase rather than reduce exchange controls. After an examination of the proposed international Bank, Mr. Aldrich concludes that there is no sound function it could undertake which could not be done better by our own existing Export-Import Bank.

Mr. Aldrich then comes to his alternative proposal. "The all-important economic problem of the post-war world is the removal of trade barriers." He proposes that the United States, the United Kingdom and other members of the British Commonwealth enter into immediate conversations on such problems as tariff barriers, imperial preference, export subsidies, bulk-purchasing and regional currency arrangements. If the proposed conference proved successful in achieving a joint agreement to shun totalitarian tactics in international trade and to adopt economic liberalism, the United States should offer to provide England "with a grant-in-aid sufficiently large to establish stability between the dollar and the pound. The sum needed may be a large one—but the problem is large and we must show courage in its solution."

Once the dollar-pound rate is stabilized, attention should be directed immediately to the stabilization of other currencies. "The prerequisites are internal political stability, a constructive solution of the problem of trade barriers, a reasonable measure of economic well-being and the absence of inflation." Implicit in all this, Mr. Aldrich concludes, is our responsibility to make our own currency in the postwar period one in which other nations can have confidence. This, as he shows, will not be easy, for it will involve the repeal of some unsound monetary legislation still on the books, and it will involve ultimately a balanced Federal budget.

There would clearly be some embarrassment in setting aside now the plans agreed to at Bretton Woods, even if they have the defects and dangers that Mr. Aldrich believes they have. It is by no means certain, either, that an Anglo-American agreement of the type he recommends could be brought about. But he has put forward a carefully reasoned argument and a constructive proposal that deserve serious open-minded study.

*Prof. John H. Williams of Harvard and vice-president of the Federal Reserve Bank of New York, in an article in **Foreign Affairs,** suggested that Congress postpone any decision on the proposed Fund, but adopt the proposed Bank with modifications. He found it to be an "unstated assumption of the Fund", among others, that there would be "a general retention of the machinery of exchange control not only for the transition period but permanently."*

11

International Money Plans

October 1, 1944

In the current issue of *Foreign Affairs*, John H. Williams, Professor of Economics at Harvard and vice president of the Federal Reserve Bank of New York, who was a critic of the proposed International Monetary Fund in its formative stages, returns to a criticism of that proposal in the form adopted at Bretton Woods. He recommends that Congress postpone any decision on the Fund at present, but makes the interesting compromise proposal that the proposed International Bank should be adopted and its functions expanded to achieve some of the ends that the Fund was intended to achieve.

Mr. Williams begins by pointing out that Congress faces a difficult dilemma. The monetary plans framed at Bretton Woods will present one of a series of major decisions about post-war international arrangements. Our action on them will be taken as an omen of things to come. If the plans are defective, we must find better ones.

"But it will not seem constructive to insist in 1945 upon some wholly new approach and to start the whole process of international negotiation over again. The realistic and helpful approach, now, whatever one's earlier preference may have been, is to see whether out of these plans, a solution can be found."

Mr. Williams suggests that it would be wise to separate the proposed Fund from the proposed Bank, to adopt the Bank with modifications and to withhold for the present a decision on the Fund. He points out that the Fund is intended, in any case, primarily as a long-run agency of monetary regulation and is unsuited to handle the transitional problems that will chiefly exist in the next few years. It would supply funds "indiscriminately to all the United Nations and would make them available on a time schedule and as a matter of automatic right." He finds it to be "an unstated assumption" of the Fund that there will be "a general retention of the machinery of exchange control not only for the transition period but permanently." This would mean a general system of foreign exchange "reporting and policing." The provisions for declaring a currency scarce and for rationing its supply would subject the United States, he holds, as the leading creditor nation, to exchange and trade discrimination. But there are no provisions for applying corrective measures to the wrong policies of debtor nations.

On the other hand, in looking for a compromise solution, Mr. Williams has become "increasingly interested since Bretton Woods in what might be accomplished through the Bank." This has led him to "wish to explore the possibilities of extending the Bank's functions to include some part of what is desired from the Fund." For the transition period, in particular, he thinks it could be the better instrument. "It would not, like the Fund, distribute foreign exchange resources indiscriminately to the many countries that do not need them as well as to those that do. It would operate selectively, and with discrimination, both as to place and to time." Mr. Williams suggests that in addition to its present intended functions there might be added to the Bank an exchange stabilization loan department. "It would require a much smaller sum and at the same time probably be much more flexible and effective than the proposed Monetary Fund."

Meanwhile, he thinks, the central post-war international economic problem will be the solution of England's special difficulties created by the $12,000,000,000 accumulation of sterling war balances in London. When this has been disposed of, the solution of monetary stabilization, he is convinced, must be found through the "key currencies" principle, and must be built upon the stabilization of the two key currencies, the dollar and the pound, with respect to each other.

While the Bretton Woods talks were going on, the countries of Europe were trying to solve their immediate currency problems individually. But Belgium, for example, was planning the unnecessary and dangerous course of deflation by reducing its outstanding note circulation by 30 or 40 per cent and freezing people's bank balances. Deflation merely brings injustices and other evils of its own, without undoing the harm of past inflation.

12

Europe's Monetary Maze

October 27, 1944

A dispatch from London to this newspaper declares that the question of the merits or demerits of the Bretton Woods world currency stabilization agreement has been pushed aside as academic in Great Britain by the more immediate and acute currency problems that threaten the liberated countries of Europe. This calls attention once more to the fact that, contrary to common belief, the proposed International Monetary Fund is planned as "a permanent institution" and is not designed to solve the currency problems of the transitional period from war to peace. It is precisely these problems, however, that are the more difficult to solve.

The boldest attempt to bring order out of chaos in the domestic currency situation has been made in Belgium. The other liberated countries of Europe are watching this experiment anxiously. Many of the details of the Belgian plan have not been made clear in the cables; but the plan in its broader outlines does not appear to be well-conceived. It aims to reverse part of the inflationary process by deflation, by reducing the outstanding note circulation by some 30 or 40 per cent, and by freezing people's present bank balances so that they can spend only a small part of them.

But once inflation has done its harm, it is impossible to try to undo this harm by the reverse policy of deflation. The deflation merely brings a new series of injustices and difficulties. Its most dangerous aspect is that by trying to force down prices and wages from the levels they have reached, it may result in economic stagnation, in unemployment, in a throttling of production. The process is politically unpopular; so much so that our London dispatch declares that the Belgian deflationary program, which is less than two weeks old, already threatens the overthrow of her present Government.

The safest policy for a Government to follow, once inflation has been allowed to occur, is to try merely to prevent the process from going further, by fixing a new value for the currency calculated to stabilize prices and wages at their new level. This means refusal to put out further issues of paper money, but it rarely involves recalling (except in exchange for new currency) part of the paper money already outstanding.

The currency problems of liberated Europe are complicated by many other factors. One of these is the system of price fixing. When prices of necessities are fixed below the levels to which the free play of supply and demand would bring them, one of two results must follow. If profit margins for producing necessities are non-existent or below the levels for producing other goods, then the commodities whose prices are fixed will either not be produced and sold, or the Government will have to subsidize the producers to make sure that they are produced and sold. In the first case shortages will be intensified in precisely the goods of which it is necessary to have fullest production. In the second case the burden on the Treasury will be greater, the budget will be thrown further out of balance by the subsidies, and more note issues, that is to say, more inflation, will be used to pay them.

Belgium today seems to be facing both consequences. The Belgian Government is sending convoys of trucks around the country to try to gather in the farm products that have not come to market. It has raised the prices paid to farmers for cattle and milk while leaving fixed retail milk and meat prices unchanged—which means that it must supply the difference by subsidies.

On humanitarian grounds and on grounds of friendliness, Americans are eager to see the newly liberated countries of Europe solve their difficult economic problems as well and as quickly as possible. They know, even on selfish grounds, that a prosperous post-war America requires a prosperous post-war Europe. But they have an even more immediate and direct interest in the policies followed by the newly liberated countries of Europe at this time. The problem of transporting and distributing American food to Europe through the Army, the Red Cross and UNRRA will be great in any case. We do not want to see it intensified by mistaken governmental policies in Europe that would reduce what the people of these countries would otherwise be able to produce for themselves.

The American Bankers Association published a carefully reasoned and conciliatory report recommending that Congress should not approve the proposed International Monetary Fund but only, with modifications, the proposed International Bank. It pointed out, among other objections, that the Fund agreement granted credit automatically as a matter of right, and did not even stipulate that its loans should be sound loans.

13

Bankers on Bretton Woods

February 5, 1945

After careful studies by several committees, the American Bankers Association has published a report in which it contends that congress should not approve the proposed International Monetary Fund, but that it should approve, with modifications, the proposed International Bank for Reconstruction and Development. The bankers recommend also an expansion of the American Government's Export-Import Bank, the repeal of the Johnson act, the removal of hampering barriers to international trade, and "the firm stabilization of the United States dollar in relation to gold."

The Association's report is well reasoned, lucidly written, and conciliatory in tone. It is clear that the authors have made every compromise that they thought could safely be made so that the proposed program might be considered with a minimum of essential changes.

The rejection of the proposed Fund is based on reasons that for the most part have already become familiar. The Fund is too big, too elaborate, too complicated, too difficult for the public to understand. The language of the agreement is so vague as to be susceptible to widely different interpretations. It grants credit automatically, as a matter of right. It does not stipulate that the loans shall be good loans. It provides no real control over the policies of borrowers. It may tempt borrowing countries to continue on the easy political path, instead of making the maximum effort to put their economic affairs in order. It threatens a repetition on a large scale of the errors we made after the First World War, when we lent too much and too carelessly. It overlooks the fact that the outside world as a whole already has more gold and dollar exchange than ever before; that our own gold stock has been going down; and that we are about to be forced to lower our legal reserve requirements. It would force us to supply dollars even to countries with which we might be having serious political differences, or countries whose trade policies discriminated against us.

The bankers believe, however, that if the proposed International Bank for Reconstruction and Development were adopted by Congress, and authorized also to make loans for the purpose of aiding countries to stabilize their currencies, it would accomplish every good purpose that the Fund would accomplish without its accompanying dangers. For the Bank agreement provides that the loans made must be for specific purposes; that they must be examined by a special committee; that they must offer promise of repayment; that the country whose currency is lent will have a veto power and that the Bank will not make loans which can be reasonably made through private channels. If the Bank were adopted, moreover, and the Fund rejected, the world would avoid the danger of jurisdictional conflicts and potential confusion and rivalry between two separate institutions. Acceptance of the Bank would also avert the psychological danger to world cooperation of a total rejection of the Bretton Woods proposals.

The American Bankers Association committees have brought in a constructive and statesmanlike report. It is to be hoped that not only Congress but the Administration itself will study the report in the same spirit.

The Administration seemed to be following slavishly the decisions of Lord Keynes and Harry Dexter White. Secretary Hans Morgenthau told a news conference that if the advice of the American Bankers Association were followed the chances were that it would kill the whole Bretton Woods Monetary Agreement. That implied that Treasury officials would take an all-or-nothing attitude before Congress regarding those agreements.

14

The Fund and the Bank

February 7, 1945

Secretary Morgenthau is reported to have told a news conference that if the advice in the recent report of the American Bankers Association were followed, "the chances are it would kill the whole Bretton Woods Monetary Agreement." He hopes, he added, that in the final analysis bankers will see "just a little further than their own immediate business."

These comments imply that Treasury officials will take an all-or-nothing attitude before Congress regarding the Bretton Woods Agreements. It may be doubted, in view of the serious objections to the proposed International Monetary Fund, whether this position will be wise. For if, in order to save the Fund, the attempt is made to tie it indissolubly to the proposed International Bank, the result may merely be that the proposed Bank itself will be rejected along with the proposed Fund. Such an outcome would be doubly unfortunate, for the desirable objectives of the Fund, without its dangers, can be better secured through the Bank. Certainly each proposal should be considered on its own merits.

It would be regrettable, also, if any attempt were made to dismiss the position of the American Bankers

Association on the ground that it reflected merely the selfish interests of bankers as such. The authors of this report are entitled to be credited with the same public spirit that animated the Treasury officials who helped to frame the Bretton Woods plan. The attribution of selfish or narrow personal motives would tend to lower the whole tone of debate and to prevent the objective consideration that the Bretton Woods plan, and every sincere criticism of it, ought to receive.

Secretary Morgenthau then declared: "It has been proved...that people in the international banking business cannot run successfully foreign exchange markets. It is up to the Governments to do it. We propose to do this if and when the legislative bodies approve Bretton Woods." Thus, though one of the clearly stated objectives of the Fund in its official text is "the elimination of foreign-exchange restrictions," President Roosevelt's Treasury Secretary announced his determination not only to impose such restrictions, but to allow no one to import or export or to draw funds to travel abroad without the government's consent.

15

Freedom of Exchange
February 10, 1945

An Associated Press report attributes to Secretary Morgenthau an interesting comment on the American Bankers Association report on the Bretton Woods agreements. "It has been proved, as far as I am concerned, that people in the international banking business cannot run successfully foreign-exchange markets. It is up to the Governments to do it. We propose to do this if and when the legislative bodies approve Bretton Woods."

Such a comment is not likely to be helpful to the Bretton Woods agreements. For those agreements have hitherto been represented as part of an effort to free the post-war foreign-exchange market from arbitrary governmental controls. One of the stated objectives of the Fund in its official text, indeed, is "the elimination of foreign-exchange restrictions." But if Secretary Morgenthau is correctly quoted, he now tells us not only that Governments are going to restrict the foreign-exchange markets, but under the agreements are going to run them entirely. This means that no one would be allowed to make a single import or export, or to use his dollars to make a trip abroad, without the Government's consent. Such an argument is hardly likely to appeal to believers in a freer world trade.

Supply creates demand. Real purchasing power grows out of production. In the aggregate, in fact, supply and demand are not merely equal but identical, since every commodity may be looked upon either as supply of its own kind or as demand for other things. The classical economists recognized this basic truth. But John Maynard Keynes (the leading author of the Bretton Woods agreements) ignored the necessary qualifications to the classical doctrine. He was confused by the existence of triangular exchange through the medium of money, and attributed every slackening of business to a shortage of "purchasing power" as measured in money. This logically led to recommendations of continuous additions to the supply of money—in other words, inflation. This Keynesian ideology permeated the Bretton Woods agreements.

16

Supply Creates Demand

February 11, 1945

One of the fallacies that have given rise to the belief that we can be saved from disaster after the war only by a continuation of huge Government spending and deficit financing is the assumption that "production" and "purchasing power" are two entirely different things. "Production" is thought of as goods, "purchasing power" as money. It is assumed that "purchasing power" must be kept above "production" if the latter is to expand. Those who believe this are finally led to the crude inflationary theory that we can keep going after the war only by the process of constantly increasing money payments regardless of production—which means constantly expanding bank credit or issuing more money from the printing presses.

Economists have long recognized the real truth of the matter. This is that purchasing power grows out of production. The great producing countries are the great consuming countries. The twentieth-century world consumes vastly more than the eighteenth-century world because it produces vastly more. Supply of wheat gives rise to demand for automobiles, radios, shoes, cotton goods, and other things that the wheat producer wants. Supply of shoes gives rise to demand for wheat, for motion pictures, for automobiles, and for other things that the shoe producer wants. In the modern world all this happens not by direct barter but by indirect exchange through the medium of money. This merely complicates, and does not change, the essential process. In the aggregate, supply and demand are not merely equal but identical, since every commodity may be looked upon either as supply of its own kind or as demand for other things.

In recent years this basic truth has been challenged by Lord Keynes among others, notably in his *General Theory of Employment, Interest and Money*, published in 1936. But Lord Keynes does not appear to have dealt with the essentials of the doctrine, but rather to have taken advantage of an error of illustration (promptly rectified) in John Stuart Mill's statement of it. This is pointed out in a reply to Keynes' criticism by Prof. Benjamin M. Anderson in *The Commercial and Financial Chronicle*. As Dr. Anderson concedes, the doctrine that supply creates its own demand assumes certain conditions. It assumes a condition of equilibrium. It assumes that the proportions among various goods and services must be right; that the terms of exchange, the price relationships, among different commodities must be right. It assumes the existence of free competition and free markets to bring about these proportions and price relations. It assumes the absence of paralyzing governmental interference with the markets.

But these necessary qualifications do not change the central truth of the doctrine. We can get post-war prosperity and full production when free enterprise and free markets are allowed to bring about the conditions of equilibrium. We do not have to keep pouring more money into the spending stream through endless Government deficits. That is not the way to sound prosperity, but the way to uncontrolled inflation.

President Roosevelt's message to Congress recommended adoption of the Bretton Woods agreements. My **Times** *editorial suggested acceptance of the proposed International Bank (with the specific power to make exchange-stabilization loans) but at least postponement of any Congressional acceptance of the Fund.*

17

Bretton Woods Proposals

February 13, 1945

The President's message to Congress on the Bretton Woods money and banking proposals is conciliatory and statesmanlike in tone. Though he recommends that Congress promptly adopt the plan both for the proposed international Bank and the proposed international Fund, he also discusses the two proposals separately, and each on its own merits.

Congress should accept the proposal for the proposed international Bank as promptly as it can do so consistent with careful study. Such action will insure two good results. It will make it possible for nations to borrow in the near future when their need for loans will be most urgent. And it will indicate to the world that the present Congress is ready to consider every proposal for international cooperation with an open mind and in a non-partisan spirit. At least one amendment to the Bank proposal, however, deserves serious consideration. This would specifically permit the Bank to make loans for currency stabilization purposes as well as for the purposes already outlined in the text of the existing Articles of Agreement.

If the Bank proposal were adopted and this amendment made, Congress could withhold for the present any decision on the Fund. The Fund is open to objections of a serious nature, some of which have already been discussed in these columns. Moreover, it becomes clear upon further study that the Fund is intended primarily as a long-run agency for monetary management. It is not adapted for dealing with some of the most serious problems in the transition period ahead. The text of the Fund Agreement itself seems to contemplate that this period of transitional arrangements will last at least five years. Once we accepted an international Bank authorized to make currency-stabilization loans, therefore, the case for postponing action on the Fund would be even stronger.

The President asks for repeal of the Johnson Act. This could be done promptly by Congress by a resolution of a few lines. The act attempts to prevent American citizens even from lending their own funds at their own risk to some of our present allies. The act has done no good and much harm. The sooner it is repealed, the sooner we will be rid of a pre-war gesture that does us no honor.

The New York State Bankers Association published a sixty-two page report on the Bretton Woods proposals, coming to substantially the same conclusions as the earlier report of the American Bankers Association: the proposed International Bank should be accepted with certain minor changes; action on the proposed Fund should be postponed; the American dollar should be maintained at a fixed value in terms of gold.

18

More on Bretton Woods

February 15, 1945

The New York State Bankers Association publishes today a sixty-two-page report on the Bretton Woods proposals prepared by its committee on international monetary matters, a group consisting of the heads of half a dozen of the leading New York City banks and of several up-State institutions. It is an important analysis, impressively argued, and comes to substantially the same conclusions as the recent report of the American Bankers Association. It holds that the proposed International Bank should be accepted with certain minor changes, but that action on the proposed International Fund should be postponed. It also urges repeal of the Johnson Act, American readiness to cooperate with Britain on the latter's financial problems, and reduction of obstacles to international trade.

The New York State Bankers conclude that the Fund is not a suitable instrumentality for dealing with the tasks that lie immediately ahead. They regard its system of credits based upon quotas as unrealistic and impractical. Another doubt as to the feasibility of the Fund arises from the lack of agreement on the interpretation of its provisions. Some of their broader conclusions follow:

The immediate task is to restore political and economic order to the world. International peace and security, internal stability in each country, and the removal of international trade barriers are the basic problems that demand attention. The establishment of the Fund prior to the restoration of favorable underlying conditions would not result in the achievement of economic stability or the elimination of exchange controls. On the contrary, we believe the Fund would tend to perpetuate exchange controls and other restrictions on the free movement of trade.

The greatest single contribution that the United States can make to world stability is to maintain the integrity of the American dollar. This can be done only by the maintenance of the fixed value of the dollar in terms of gold and the attainment as soon as practicable of a sound national budget and other sound internal policies. The adoption of a trade policy greatly reducing restrictions on United States imports would also contribute to world stability.

These conclusions emerge from a careful report the whole text of which merits serious study. The New York State Bankers point out that the proposed International Bank, with some additional authority, could accomplish nearly all the desired objectives of the proposed Fund without the latter's dangers.

Private bankers and technical experts were opposed to the provisions of the proposed International Fund because they were convinced that "the divergence of conditions in the various countries is so great that the stabilization of each currency must be treated as an individual problem" and not by a "formula that can be applied to all cases."

19

The Bretton Woods Bill

February 17, 1945

It is to be hoped that the bill on the Bretton Woods agreements now introduced in Congress will be considered in an open-minded and nonpartisan spirit. Special provisions added by the bill will need to be examined in addition to those of the Bretton Woods agreements themselves. The main question to be asked now is whether, under the bill as drawn, Congress will be free to consider particular provisions of the Bretton Woods agreements on their individual merits.

Technical experts, including those of the American Bankers Association and other bodies representing the bankers of the country, have urged that the proposed International Bank be adopted as a helpful instrument in world economic cooperation. But they have put forward strong reasons for at least postponing until a later time action on the proposed International Fund. As the New York State Bankers Association committee remarked this week in connection with the Fund:

> We are convinced that the divergence of conditions in the various countries is so great that

the stabilization of each currency must be treated as an individual problem. We do not think it is possible to develop a workable formula that can be applied to all cases. Too much depends upon the will and the efforts of the individual country for the over-all approach to achieve the success anticipated by the authors of the Monetary Plan.

The judgment of these bankers ought certainly not be rejected out of hand. As a group, bankers want to see as high a volume as possible of international trade. They want stable exchanges so that they and their business customers can grant international credits and conduct other international transactions with reasonable security. The cause of international cooperation would itself only be hurt in the long run if unwise measures which would work out badly are adopted along with necessary measures which have a high prospect of success.

There were still major obscurities surrounding the Monetary Fund agreement. Many Americans still believe that the agreement took us back along the road to a gold standard and currency stability, but Lord Keynes, leader of the British delegation at Bretton Woods, had declared before the House of Lords that "this Bretton Woods plan is the exact opposite of...a gold standard", and that it would permit both "flexible" and discriminatory exchange-rates. The Roosevelt Administration should have withdrawn the Fund proposal until these ambiguities had been cleared up.

20

Money Plan Obscurities

March 15, 1945

This newspaper received a letter from Robert Boothby, which it published on March 4, and a second letter, which it published on March 14, referring to the Bretton Woods agreements. Mr. Boothby is a Member of Parliament and chairman of the Monetary Policy Committee in London.

In both letters Mr. Boothby pointed to what he called certain "major obscurities" in the Bretton Woods Monetary Fund agreement, and he pointed out that regarding several of them precisely the opposite interpretations had been made in Great Britain from those generally made here:

> You have been led to believe that the Bretton Woods proposals take us all back along the road to a gold standard, currency stability, non-discrimination and multilateral trade. We have been assured that they constitute the exact reverse of a gold standard, that exchange rates will be flexible and that reciprocal trade agreements involving discrimination will be permissible.

Treasury spokesmen, discussing Mr. Boothby's contentions before the House Banking and Currency Committee, do not appear to have dealt with them very satisfactorily. They questioned Mr. Boothby's motives and his purpose in being in this country at this time. Such personal considerations do not meet the real issue, which is, Do the obscurities and ambiguities which Mr. Boothby alleges to be in the Bretton Woods agreement in fact exist?

There can be not the slightest doubt that they do. Widely different interpretations have been made of the Fund agreement here and in London. It was Lord Keynes, leader of the British delegation at Bretton Woods, who declared before the House of Lords: "If I have any authority to pronounce on what is and what is not the essence and meaning of a gold standard, I should say that this plan is the exact opposite of it." It is Lord Keynes, also, who in a letter to *The Times* of London contended that the Bretton Woods plans would still permit Britain to make purely regional trade and currency arrangements, a view that has been disputed in the United States. There has developed in addition a vital difference of opinion concerning whether the credit granted by the Fund is automatic, regardless of unsound currency or other economic policies in the borrowing countries, or whether the Fund has a right to withhold credit because of such policies.

Wholly apart from Mr. Boothby's personal motives, in short, he is correct when he writes that "Nothing could be more deleterious to the future of Anglo-American relations than that the two countries should sign an agreement, each thinking that it means something quite different." It simply does not make sense for the United States, Great Britain or any other country to commit itself to the Bretton Woods Fund agreement without knowing precisely what it has committed itself to.

Yet a strange situation has arisen in recent months. It is the bankers and others who are critical of the Bretton Woods Fund Agreement—in part, precisely because they fear that it really is "the exact opposite" of the gold standard—who are today being denounced in some quarters as "isolationists" and enemies of international cooperation. It is some of the very people who are insisting on the Bretton Woods Fund Agreement, on the other hand, many of them precisely because they believe that it will permit the continuance of managed inconvertible paper money systems, who try to arrogate to themselves alone' the title of "internationalists."

This strange paradox is brought out in a review in the current *Political Science Quarterly* of Prof. Edwin W. Kemmerer's book, "Gold and the Gold Standard." As Professor Kemmerer points out, the most international standard is gold, while the most national is paper or some other non-gold currency.

A nation that formerly adhered to the international gold standard, it is true, did not sign any formal document of monetary cooperation with other nations, but the cooperation was none the less real and thoroughgoing. A nation that wished to stay on the gold standard had to keep its own currency stable in terms of gold. To do this it had to make its currency convertible on demand into a definite and fixed quantity of gold. To make sure that its promise of convertibility would be kept, it had to keep its budget in reasonable balance and see to it that an inflationary expansion of bank credit did not take place within its borders. It had to allow freedom of gold export. To make sure that this did not drain it of gold, it had to maintain a two-sided trade balance. It could not take its economy so far out of line with the world economy as to cut off its exports and take in too great an excess of imports.

There are several ways in which the problem might be dealt with. Congress might accept the Fund subject to an explicit set of understandings or interpretations on essential points at present left in obscurity. A much better course in every respect, however, would be for the Administration to withdraw the Fund proposal at this time, to ask Congress to adopt now only the much less controversial Bank proposal, and then to attempt to reach an agreement with the British on the important points at present subject to such divergent interpretations. An agreement so arrived at could be submitted to other nations for comments or suggestions. This would be a far wiser course than the Administration will pursue if it insists that Congress adopt the present Fund agreement blindly, without this essential clarification.

The international gold standard, when it prevailed, represented the closest form of international economic and monetary cooperation that the modern world has ever achieved. Through it the value of each nation's currency was tied in with all the rest. Yet at this point, incredibly, the advocates of continued nationally-managed inconvertible paper money systems called themselves the only true believers in "international cooperation."

21

Gold vs. Nationalism
March 17, 1945

The monetary plan embodied in the Bretton Woods agreements, Lord Keynes assured the House of Lords, is "the exact opposite" of the gold standard. Now the international gold standard, when it was in its fullest operation in the early part of the present century, represented the closest form of international economic and monetary cooperation that the modern world has ever achieved. Through it the value of each nation's currency was tied in with that of all the rest. Through it, likewise, each nation's economy was tied in with that of the rest of the world.

Yet a strange situation has arisen in recent months. It is the bankers and others who are critical of the Bretton Woods Fund Agreement—in part, precisely because they fear that it really is "the exact opposite" of the gold standard—who are today being denounced in some quarters as "isolationists" and enemies of international cooperation. It is some of the very people who are insisting on the Bretton Woods Fund Agreement, on the other hand, many of them precisely because they believe that it will permit the continuance of managed inconvertible paper money systems, who try to arrogate to themselves alone the title of "internationalists."

This strange paradox is brought out in a review in the current *Political Science Quarterly* of Prof. Edwin W. Kemmerer's book, "Gold and the Gold Standard." As Professor Kemmerer points out, the most international standard is gold, while the most national is paper or some other non-gold currency.

A nation that formerly adhered to the international gold standard, it is true, did not sign any formal document of monetary cooperation with other nations, but the cooperation was none the less real and thoroughgoing. A nation that wished to stay on the gold standard had to keep its own currency stable in terms of gold. To do this it had to make its currency convertible on demand into a definite and fixed quantity of gold. To make sure that its promise of convertibility would be kept, it had to keep its budget in reasonable balance and see to it that an inflationary expansion of bank credit did not take place within its borders. It had to allow freedom of gold export. To make sure that this did not drain it of gold, it had to maintain a two-sided trade balance. It could not take its economy so far out of line with the world economy as to cut off its exports and take in too great an excess of imports.

It is precisely because the gold standard did have these international implications that nationalists, and the advocates of domestic managed economies and of autarchy, were so opposed to it. It is no accident that the literature of nazism is so full of denunciations of the gold standard and of "international bankers." But now, in a topsy-turvy argument, it is the bankers who are being denounced, not as internationalists but as "isolationists," because they prefer a restoration of the international gold standard to a system under which each nation individually would be free to follow whatever unsound policies it wished, while the nations collectively would have to bail it out of the difficulties into which it fell as a consequence.

In an inconsistent report that read like a compromise arrived at in order to obtain agreement among all fourteen members, the Committee for Economic Development, a group of businessmen, pointed out the dangers of putting the Fund (as then planned) under pressure to make long-term loans, to do it whether or not these loans were likely to be repaid, and to do it without having the power even to lay down conditions for such loans. The CED recommended that powers to make long and short-term stabilization loans be made merely discretionary and turned over to the proposed International Bank. But the CED inconsistently recommended that the Fund be retained, even after it had thus been made unnecessary.

22

The CED on Bretton Woods

March 25, 1945

The research committee of the group of outstanding business men known as the Committee for Economic Development has published a statement on the Bretton Woods proposals. This statement reads like a compromise arrived at in order to obtain agreement from all fourteen members of the committee. As often happen with such compromises, the position taken lacks clarity and embodies some inner contradictions.

The committee fears, quite properly, that as the agreements stand at present the principal demands upon the International Monetary Fund will come, not from temporary imbalances of trade, "but from the very serious distortions in production and international trade relations caused by the war." It fears that great pressure will be put upon the management of the Fund to make what will be in effect long-term loans, to do it whether these loans are likely to be repaid or not, and to do it without having the power even to lay down the conditions under which the loans are made. It suggests, therefore, that establishment of the Fund be postponed unless the International Bank is given the express power, which it does not have at present, to make "loans for long-term and short-term stabilization purposes." If the Bank were granted this power, the committee argues, the managers of the Fund would be relieved of this pressure, because they could then "refer to the Bank those transactions for which the Fund is not intended," and the Bank would be able to require a country to correct unsound policies in return for the loan.

The committee is right in wishing to give the Bank this power to make stabilization loans. The American Bankers Association also made this recommendation. But the ABA report, as well as that of the New York State Bankers Association, pointed out that if the proposed International Bank were granted this power, the Fund would then become unnecessary. It is difficult to understand why the CED committee recommends retaining the Fund, particularly as it is now drawn up, once the International Bank has been granted this new power. There would be no important function left for the Fund to perform, and it is not drawn up to perform its proposed functions well.

The first requirement of any International Monetary Fund, if it is to be adopted, is that it should be drawn up on the same basic principle as the proposed International Bank. The managers of the Fund should retain the right of discretion at all times. They should be able to insist, whenever they think it necessary, that a nation having access to the resources of the Fund should put and keep its own financial house in order—that it should, for example, refrain from discriminatory trade practices, or the imposition of unreasonable barriers on trade, that it stop an inflationary expansion of bank credit or the printing of paper money, or take steps to balance its budget. Unless the Fund has the clear authority to insist upon such conditions in return for its loans, its resources will be dissipated to no purpose or to harmful purposes, and it will never accomplish the objects that its advocates hope for from it.

The CED committee itself lays it down as one of "five basic principles" that "loans should be truly loans; currency transactions should be currency transactions; and gifts should be gifts. Lack of clarity as between intent and method at this point will produce...misunderstandings and bitterness between countries. If a gift cannot be made as a gift, it should not mask behind the facade of a loan." On this principle alone the Fund as it is at present drawn is unsatisfactory. But if the proposed International Bank is granted the power to make discretionary long-term or short-term stabilization loans, as the CED committee recommends, the Fund will not be necessary.

The small block of "silver Senators" tried to get the Bretton Woods agreements to include "world recognition of silver as a monetary metal." Had they succeeded they would have postponed even further any return to an international gold standard—the one step that would have restored stable exchanges and end the chaos of nationally "managed" currencies.

23

Silver Boys in Bretton Woods

April 7, 1945

In the last dozen years the "silver Senators" have had a political influence fantastically out of proportion to their numbers or to the interests they represent. These Senators come from only a small handful of States. Silver production is a very minor source of the income even of these states. For the country as a whole it accounts for less than one-twentieth of 1 per cent of the national income. Yet the silver bloc in Congress has insisted upon and obtained measures forcing the Treasury to buy huge stocks of unneeded silver. These were bought far above the market price from domestic producers and at an artificially boosted price from foreign holders. The result has been an inexcusable waste of the public funds. Incidentally, the policy did great harm to the economy of China, about which the silver Senators had professed to be especially solicitous.

Now some of the silver Senators are turning their attention toward the Bretton Woods agreements. What they see in them principally seems to be one more opportunity to "do something for silver." They want "world recognition of silver as a monetary metal."

Misgivings have been expressed regarding the proposed International Monetary Fund. One reason for these misgivings is that the Fund as at present conceived may postpone rather than expedite a return to the international gold standard. Only to the extent that the international gold standard is eventually restored is the world likely in the long run to have stable exchanges, a great volume of international trade, and a final escape from the chaos of nationally "managed" currencies. The injection of the silver issue would merely delay such a result and further confuse public thought. The exchange rate of a nation on a silver standard would necessarily fluctuate constantly in relation to those nations on a gold standard. Bimetallism or symmetallism, on the other hand, would merely introduce needless complications and a new controversial issue at a time when we particularly need to avoid as many controversial issues as possible. possible.

Some amendments are needed if the Bretton Woods agreements are to accomplish the ends that their sponsors have in view. But these amendments should be designed to simplify the agreements, not to complicate them. No amendment is likely to be in the right direction unless it is sincere and disinterested. There can be no excuse for amendments merely calculated to embarrass the working of the agreements, or designed to appease some selfish interest or pressure group.

The agreements signed at Bretton Woods would end by creating more chaos in international trade and economic relations, not less. Under the old gold standard each country was responsible for keeping its own currency sound. Under the Bretton Woods system, an international Fund would be forced to buy depreciated currencies far above their market values, regardless of the reasons for the depreciation. The provision for uniform proportionate devaluation was a provision for periodic world inflation. The system was designed "to make resort to inflation easy, smooth, and above all respectable."

The Bretton Woods Agreements also contemplated international commodity controls. There were the strongest reasons to fear that these would mean a revival and extension on a far greater scale of the type of commodity controls of the Thirties, which mainly resulted in disastrous failures.

The agreements, in short, pretended to provide for a future of "international cooperation", but what they provided for instead was a future of increased State domination and control over economic life. The bleak prospect was that the individual's "living standards will decline with his liberties."

The following article, subtitled "Free Trade or State Domination?", is reprinted from *The American Scholar,* Winter, 1944/5.

24

The Coming Economic
World Pattern

Winter, 1944/45

Freedom of trade, in the eyes of Adam Smith and his nineteenth-century successors in the liberal tradition, meant freedom from government interference. All that the "classical" economists asked of governments in the field of international trade was that they should *permit it to occur*. They wanted a removal of prohibitions and of nearly all tariffs. But they did not ask for positive "encouragement" or artificial stimulants. They were as much opposed to bounties as they were to barriers.

What the older liberals meant by freedom, in short, was freedom of the individual citizen. They asked that he be free to sell his goods to whatever country and whatever market would pay him the best price for them. They asked that he be free to buy whatever he wanted wherever he could get it cheapest. They argued that these freedoms were not only good in themselves, but that they represented by far the best means to bring about the most efficient division of labor and to maximize world production and world consumption. All they asked of government was that it enforce the laws against fraud, force, and theft, and that it refrain from debasing the currency.

The world barriers to international trade in the nineteen-thirties, for which every large nation was in part responsible, but in the erection of which the totalitarian governments went to the greatest lengths, brought about such chaos that few responsible persons now undertake to defend them. High tariffs, import quotas, export subsidies, competitive currency depreciation, blocked currencies, bilateral arrangements, forced barter—all these are today deplored by lip in all respectable circles. The demand now is for International Cooperation.

I

But when the concrete proposals for this international cooperation are examined, it turns out to be something radically different from the international cooperation hoped for by the older liberals. It is not the freedom of the private citizens of any country to trade with the private citizens of any other. It is not primarily the cooperation among private citizens of different countries at all. It is primarily cooperation among governments. As in the thirties, it is governments that are going to take the matter in hand. But instead, as in the wicked thirties, of restricting trade and making economic war upon each other, this time, we are told, the governments are going to direct and stimulate trade in the interests of peace.

It is a pleasant fantasy; but there are the gravest reasons for doubting that it will ever be realized. There are the strongest reasons, on the other hand, for fearing that this kind of intergovernmental cooperation will break down, and that when it does the resulting chaos in international trade and economic relations will be greater than ever.

For government officials, even when they really understand (which is very rarely) the basic economic forces that they are trying to control, are almost never disinterested. They are almost certain to reflect the special interests of some political pressure group. The interests of the pressure groups represented by the bureaucrats of one nation are certain to clash with those of the pressure groups represented by the bureaucrats of another. And these conflicting interests, precisely because they are represented by their respective governments, are far more likely to clash openly, directly, and politically than in a world of genuine free trade.

But perhaps, before we come back to these larger issues, it would be well to examine in detail the leading proposals so far put forward for the postwar economic world.

The agreements reached by the experts at Bretton Woods seem to typify the intended shape of things to come. The proposed International Monetary Fund has as one of its ostensible purposes the promotion of "exchange stability." Now the way to secure exchange stability, as worked out before the first World War, was clear. A nation kept its own currency sound.

It made it convertible on demand into a definite and fixed quantity of gold. To make sure that the promise to pay that fixed quantity of gold would be kept, it saw to it that there was not an excessive expansion of bank credit. It saw to it also that the central government did not issue such a volume of debt that its ability to maintain interest on that debt and to retire it would come into question. A nation saw to it that the government's bonds were sold to the public, so that they were paid for out of real savings and not merely out of the creation of additional bank credit. If a government were to meet all these requirements it had to balance its budget, or at least make certain that its budget was not too long or too heavily out of balance.

When the public was confident, as a result of these conditions, that the promise of gold-convertibility would be kept, a nation's currency in the foreign exchange market was stabilized (with comparatively minute fluctuations) in terms of this fixed gold value. The currencies of other countries were likewise fixed in terms of definite gold values. As each currency was held, by each country's own policy, to the value of a fixed quantity of gold, it followed that each gold currency was necessarily fixed in terms of every other. General exchange stability was preserved.

This was the international gold standard. It was a form of international cooperation worked out and perfected through the centuries. It reached its highest development in the latter part of the nineteenth century and in the present century before the first World War.

II

One will look in vain through the Articles of Agreement on the International Monetary Fund for any reference to balanced budgets, to limitations on internal credit expansion, or to any definite requirement for gold convertibility. How, then, does the Fund propose to maintain international currency stability? Instead of contemplating that each currency shall be separately anchored to gold, and that each nation shall be responsible for maintaining that link so far as its own currency is concerned, the Fund proposes that every currency be tied directly to every other.

This is to be done by forcing the strong currencies automatically to support the weaker.

Suppose, to take a fictitious example, that the Ruritanian rurita has a par value of twenty cents in terms of American dollars. Suppose it has a sinking spell, or that everybody shows a sudden desire to get rid of ruritas and to acquire dollars instead. It becomes the duty of the Fund to supply these dollars, at least up to an amount stipulated in advance in the Articles of Agreement. The Fund must keep buying the ruritas at twenty cents. It must do this regardless of whether the rurita is sinking because the Ruritanians are buying more goods from the outside world than they have the exports or credit to pay for, or because Ruritania is having a revolution, or because it has a Fascist government that has just announced that it is expropriating the property of some minority group, or because it has a budget deficit brought about by a heavy armament program, or simply because it is grinding out too much paper money on its printing presses.

Now the real value of the rurita, left to the natural play of supply and demand, may be only two cents. Nevertheless, it must continue to be bought by the Fund at twenty cents. But if, as is most probable, it is being bought by dollars, this means that American taxpayers are buying two cent ruritas for twenty cents, thereby immediately losing 90 per cent of their investment on each purchase, while they pay for Ruritania's luxury imports, her armament program, or her Fascist experiment.

But does the International Monetary Fund, though it explicitly lists that objective among its purposes, even contemplate exchange stability? On the contrary, it clearly contemplates a great deal of exchange instability. It provides, first of all, that any nation may at any time devalue its currency 10 per cent. It is explicitly stipulated that "the Fund shall raise no objection." Any nation may propose a devaluation of its currency by another 10 per cent, and the Fund must either concur or object within seventy-two hours. The practical effect of this pressure for a quick answer will be to give the benefit of the doubt to the nation that wants to devaluate. If a nation wishes to devalue its currency even further, it must consult the Fund. But if the Fund refuses its request the member can simply withdraw, without advance notice, if it prefers further devaluation to whatever additional automatic credit it might still be entitled to in the Fund.

But the most ominous provision of the Fund, from an inflationary standpoint, is that which permits it by a majority of the total voting power to make "uniform proportionate changes in the par values of the currencies of all members." Each such change must be approved also by every member that has 10 per cent or more of the total of the quotas. It is true that an individual member of the Fund, if it decides within seventy-two hours, may be allowed to keep the par value of its currency unchanged; but as devaluation of all other currencies would be certain to cause a prompt drop of commodity prices within a non-devaluing nation, all nations would be virtually forced to participate in the devaluation.

Now this provision of the Fund is a provision for periodic world inflation. The historic instances in which the par value of the monetary unit has been increased are so rare as to be negligible. The practical political pressures are always in the other direction. So we are safe in assuming that the "uniform propor-

tionate changes" referred to by the Fund mean
uniform proportionate *devaluations*. Devaluation is
the modern euphemism for debasement of the
coinage. It always means repudiation. It means that
the promise to pay a certain definite weight of gold
has been broken, and that the devaluing government,
for its bonds or currency notes, will pay a smaller
weight of gold.

III

When a nation devalues by acting alone, all this is
plain enough. Foreigners who hold bank deposits in
that nation, or exchange bills drawn on that nation,
or any obligation of that nation stated in terms of its
own currency, know that they have been cheated.
The value of their claims in terms of their own currency immediately drops by the percentage of the
devaluation. They will be paid only 90 or 80 or 50
cents on the dollar. All this makes devaluation
morally embarrassing to the devaluing nation.

There are other embarrassing effects. Devaluation
seldom comes out of a clear sky. It follows an overexpansion of the government's debt or currency notes
or an overexpansion of internal bank credit.
Foreigners, reading these signs, begin to withdraw
their deposits. The nation's own citizens, seeking to
protect their own position, begin to transfer their
deposits to other countries that look safer. This is
called the flight of capital. The politicians in power,
and economic writers who reflect their point of view,
seek to put the blame, not on the government that
has made its credit and intentions questionable, but
on the creditors who question them. They call the

money of these creditors hot money—though it is, of course, merely money that is trying to leave hot places. In spite of this modern vocabulary, nations are still embarrassed by this flight of capital and this public evidence of distrust. Moreover, it is a blow to national pride and prestige for a nation's currency to sell at a discount in the foreign exchange markets.

It is obvious that a *uniform* depreciation of *all* currencies would either remove or conceal most of these embarrassing results to any single government. Though the dollar, say, would go to a discount of 25 or 50 per cent, the man in the street would hardly suspect it at first because all the external measuring rods would have shrunk in exact proportion. A hundred dollars would still be worth the same number of pounds, francs, marks, lire, rubles, and so on, as before, and vice versa, because they would be different pounds, francs, and rubles, as well as dollars. Relative foreign exchange rates would remain unchanged. There would be no flight of capital, because every place to which it could go would be equally disadvantageous. The provision in the Fund for world inflation, in brief, is a provision to make resort to inflation easy, smooth, and, above all, respectable.

But the real harm that inflation would do would be no less under world-wide inflation than under national inflation. Commodity prices would rise. Everybody's cost of living would go up. Those who lived on pensions, either private or part of government social security systems, would find them buying less than before. The holders of government securities would find the real value of their securities greatly cut. All those with fixed incomes would find themselves subjected to an invisible but real and ungraduated income tax (in addition to the govern-

134

ment's acknowledged graduated income tax.) All those with savings accounts and insurance policies would find them cut by an invisible but real and uniform capital levy. In short, private citizens, as before, would be cheated by their governments; but the government propaganda agencies would assure them that the latest inflation had merely ushered in a new paradise.

The proposed International Monetary Fund is bad from so many aspects that it is difficult to know in advance which danger will prove the most serious. By keeping up exchange rates by artificial means, buying currencies at par regardless of their real market value, and making devaluation easy and respectable, the way will be cleared for encouraging every government in power to follow the easy political path. Any government could continue to pay heavy subsidies to all sorts of pressure groups, to embark on public works and patronage on a grand scale, and to tax lightly, thus continuing chronic budget deficits and financing them by added debt.

But all this will not give us free exchange markets. The Fund Agreement does not say in so many words whether there will be a free foreign exchange market or not. But it provides for the continuance of controls during an indefinite "transition" period, and it encourages permanent controls over capital movements. To control international capital movements would in practice require supervision and and policing of all exchange transactions. In practice, therefore, people could not buy or sell abroad, or travel, without going through a great maze of red tape to get permission from their government to do so. They would lose the power to dispose of their property as they wished, or to emigrate and take their money with them. Government power over the lives and actions of its citizens would be extended in yet further directions. Still more former freedoms would be abridged or circumscribed.

IV

Let us turn from the proposed International Monetary Fund to the proposed International Bank for Reconstruction and Development. Here at least is an institution in which, with proper safeguards, the possibilities for good might outweigh the possibilities for harm. The Bank, apart from its unncessarily large subscribed capital ($9,100,000,000), is set up on a comparatively conservative basis. It is not to lend or guarantee loans for more than the full amount of its unimpaired subscribed capital, reserves and surplus. It is not to make loans on an automatic basis, like the Fund. It can exercise discretion. A project, for example, for which funds are being asked must be deemed meritorious by a committee selected by the Bank. The borrower must be "in position to meet its obligations."

Such a Bank, in the decade immediately following the war, could perform a useful service. In particular, it could make loans to stabilize their currency to those nations that show a genuine will and capacity to do so. Whether the proposed International Bank would provide a better medium for this purpose than the existing American Export-Import Bank is a question of practical judgment. The International Bank would have the advantage of symbolizing international cooperation. There would be psychological and political advantages in making individual nations responsible for payment of their debts to a Bank

136

representing forty-five different nations rather than to a bank merely representing one. On the other hand, while the United States would supply the lion's share of the lendable funds of such a Bank, and probably assume an even greater share of the risks, and while most of the loans would doubtless be floated in this market, our government would have much less to say about the loans and the conditions attached to them than if it were making them alone. While it is true that the American representative on the Bank would be technically free to veto a proposed loan made in dollars in this market, it might be made very embarrassing for him to do this.

It is not necessary here to weigh the relative merits of the proposed International Bank and our existing Export-Import Bank as a medium for making international stabilization loans. But it is important to point out that there are only two sound reasons why governments, either individually or jointly, should engage at this time in the business of international lending at all. The first is the whole record of default and repudiation of foreign loans in the inter-war period. This was brought about to some extent by real embarrassment on the part of debtors, but even more by the prevailing anti-foreign and anti-capitalistic ideology which regards the foreign lender, not as a man who takes risks and supplies essential aid, but as an "exploiter" who "throttles" the native economy. This record of default and repudiation has led to at least a temporary reluctance of private investors to make further foreign loans. The second reason why government intervention is now needed is that the terrific disruption brought about by war will make it extremely difficult for some nations to stabilize their currencies without outside help.

But whatever governmental institutions are used to make such loans should be temporary in nature. They should confine themselves to currency stabilization loans only. Where help is needed for humanitarian reasons it should be granted freely and generously, as a pure gift. The United Nations Relief and Rehabilitation Administration already exists for this purpose. Its scope may need to be expanded. But everything above this should be placed on a strictly business basis. It will never be placed on such a basis if it is managed by governments. Where loans are made by private groups, risking their own funds, they will be made, in the overwhelming main, where the risks seem smallest and the chance of profit greatest. Under these conditions world resources are likely to be utilized in the most efficient manner. But where loans are made by government officials who risk other people's funds and not their own, they are bound to be made primarily for political reasons and will often be wasteful from an economic point of view.

It is contemplated that the loans guaranteed by the proposed International Bank will be guaranteed first of all by some government. If the project for which the loan is made is located in Ruritania, for example, the Ruritanian government or central bank would have to guarantee the loan before the International Bank would do so. This would, of course, reduce the risk assumed by the International Bank. On the other hand, it would enable it to make loans only to projects that had home government support. The home government, by this power to give or refuse guarantees, would exercise a great influence on the development and direction of home industry. It would be in a stronger position than otherwise to grant or withhold political favors. It is important to

138

keep in mind that a government would be less likely to think of the broad economic effects of such loans than of their effects in increasing the potential armament program or the economic self-efficiency of their country in time of war. These considerations, however, would not be the same as those that would lead to the most efficient utilization of world resources. Quite the contrary.

V

I have dwelt at length upon the proposed International Fund and Bank because these are specific proposals that have already been presented in detail. Space unfortunately does not permit an adequate analysis of the proposals for international commodity controls in the postwar period. At the moment of writing only one of these—the Anglo-American oil agreement—has reached the stage of presentation to the public. But indications from many sides have already made it clear that what is being contemplated is a revival and extension on a far greater scale of the type of international commodity controls of the thirties. This seems likely to apply, if the planners have their way, to cotton, wheat, sugar, coffee, tin, beef, tea, rubber, wool, copper, nitrates, cocoa, and quinine. Controls for some of these existed before the war. Many of these peacetime controls have merely been allowed to remain dormant.

The chief controls have proved disastrous failures. Almost invariably they follow the same general pattern. Ostensibly the effort always is merely to "stabilize" the price of the commodity. But in every instance (except in one or two where a temporary control has been imposed by some single, powerful governmental buyer) the interests of the producers have been put first. The result in every such instance is that the price is fixed above the level that market conditions justify. To compensate for this, a proportional restriction of output is usually placed on each producer subject to the control. This has several immediately bad effects. It means that total world production is cut. The world's consumers are able to enjoy less of that product than they would have enjoyed without restriction. The world is just that much poorer. Consumers are forced to pay higher prices than otherwise for that product. They have just that much less to spend on other products.

A uniform proportional restriction means, on the one hand, that the efficient low-cost producers are not permitted to turn out all of the output that they can at a low price.

It means, on the other hand, that the inefficient high-cost producers are artificially kept in business. This increases the average cost of producing the product. It is being produced less efficiently than otherwise. The inefficient marginal producer thus artificially kept in that line of production continues to tie up land, labor, and capital that could much more profitably and efficiently be devoted to other uses.

If this artificial restriction of output does not take place, unsold surpluses of the over-priced commodity continue to pile up until the market for that product finally collapses to a far greater extent than if the control program had never been put into effect. Or producers outside the restriction program, stimulated by the artificial rise in price, expand their own production enormously. This is what happened to the British rubber restriction and the American cotton restriction programs. In either case the collapse of

140

prices finally goes to catastrophic lengths that would never have been reached without the restriction scheme. The plan that started out so bravely to "stabilize" prices and conditions brings incomparably greater *instability* than the free forces of the market could possibly have brought.

Of course the international commodity controls after the war, we are told, are going to avoid all these errors. This time prices are going to be fixed that are "fair" not only for producers but for consumers. Producing and consuming nations are going to agree on just what these fair prices are, because no one will be unreasonable. Fixed prices will necessarily involve "just" allotments and allocations for production and consumption among nations, but only cynics will anticipate any unseemly international disputes regarding these. Finally, by the greatest miracle of all, this postwar world of super-international controls and coercions is also going to be a world of "free" international trade!

Just what the planners mean by free trade in this connection I am not sure, but we can be sure of some of the things they do not mean. They do not mean the freedom of ordinary people to buy and sell, lend and borrow, at whatever prices or rates they like and wherever they find it most profitable to do so. They do not mean the freedom of the plain citizen to raise as much of a given crop as he wishes, to come and go at will, to settle where he pleases, to take his capital and other belongings with him. They mean, I suspect, the freedom of bureaucrats to settle these matters for him. And they tell him that if he docilely obeys the bureaucrats he will be rewarded by a rise in his living standards. But if the planners succeed in tying up the idea of international cooperation with the idea of increased State domination and control over economic life, the international controls of the future seem only too likely to follow the pattern of the past, in which case the plain man's living standards will decline with his liberties.

Part II
Aftermath

25

Excerpts from "Will Dollars Save the World?"*

There is a widespread belief that the United States has a duty to lend or give huge sums to other countries, principally in Europe, if it is to save the world from communism and chaos. This belief is held almost as strongly in the United States, which would make the sacrifices, as it is in the European countries that are expected to benefit from them.

In its most widely held form the conclusion rests on the assumption that the present economic difficulties of Europe are in the main the consequences of the destruction and dislocations of war. It is assumed that there is a definite deficit that America can make up by loans or gifts, that America must supply this if Europe is to recover, that Europe's economic recovery is essential for America's prosperity, and that therefore it is "good business" for America to make these gifts or loans, even if the loans are never repaid. The sacrifices in the present, it is argued, will be more than compensated by gains in the future.

*Published in 1947 by The Foundation for Economic Education, Irvington-on-Hudson, New York. A 6,500-word condensation was published in the January, 1948, issue of *The Reader's Digest* and in all its foreign issues of that month.

This set of assumptions found expression in the celebrated speech of General George C. Marshall, the American Secretary of State, at Harvard on June 5, 1947:

> The truth of the matter is that Europe's requirements, for the next three or four years, of foreign food and other essential products—principally from America—are so much greater than her present ability to pay that she must have substantial additional help, or face economic, social and political deterioration of a very grave character.

The implication of this statement is that Europe's shortages are being imposed upon her by conditions beyond her control, and that the present import surplus of Europe is solely the result of these shortages and not of other factors. This is also the contention that runs throughout the report of sixteen European nations on the Marshall plan.

It would be ungenerous and short-sighted to minimize the appalling physical destruction and the enormous economic and political problems that the last World War brought upon Europe. We can never forget that in the war against Nazism England stood for a whole year alone. Thousands of her houses and factories were destroyed by blitz. Her peacetime equipment ran down. Her export trade was reduced to less than a third. Most of her foreign investments had to be sold.

Yet when all this has been admitted, we must go on to ask ourselves in all candor whether it is the destruction and dislocations of the war or the governmental policies followed since that war which are primarily responsible for the present European crisis.

146

And whatever we decide regarding the causes of the present crisis, we must also keep in mind that the central question we have now to answer is not what caused it, but what measures and policies are most likely to cure it. Our real problem is not the past, but the future.

Let us begin, therefore, by taking a closer look at the existing situation in Europe.

The main obstacles to European recovery are the present economic policies followed by the governments of Europe.

When a currency is overvalued (to consider the harmful effects of merely one governmental control) it produces a *chronic* surplus of imports over exports. The overvaluation of the currency tends, on the other hand, to make the prices of that nation's imports cheaper than they would otherwise be in terms of that currency. This naturally encourages people in that nation to increase their purchases of imports. The overvaluation of the currency tends, on the other hand, to make the prices of that nation's exports high in terms of other currencies. This discourages other countries from buying.

Suppose, for example, that a French brandy sells in Paris for 1,200 francs a bottle. The black-market rate for the franc is about 280 to the dollar as this is being written [in 1946]. Let us assume that in a free market the franc would sell a little higher—say about 240 to the dollar. At such a rate the brandy could be bought for $5 a bottle in American money. But the official rate for the French franc, which the American importer is now forced to pay, is 119 to the dollar. This means that the brandy must cost him more than $10 a bottle. The arbitrary exchange rate enforced by the French police raises the price as much as would a

100 per cent American import duty (on top of the duty that we actually impose). And this applies to every French export to this country. Is it surprising, apart from any other factor, that France is exporting so relatively little to us?

In the same way, if we look at the problem from the other side, a typewriter that costs $100 in the United States would cost a French buyer, if he had to pay 240 francs for the dollar, 24,000 francs. But as he is able, thanks to exchange control and American loans, to get the dollar for only 119 francs, the typewriter costs him less than 12,000 francs. And this applies to every American export to France. Is it surprising that Frenchmen should want to buy a great deal from us?

Because the overvaluation of the franc makes French goods expensive in terms of dollars, the would-be French exporter may have to reduce his price in terms of francs if he is to meet the competition of other sellers, foreign or American, in the American market. Yet he may see no reason for doing this, because he can realize a larger margin of profit on his domestic sales. And inflation at home, by causing a rise in domestic money incomes, will cause a rising home demand for goods which otherwise would be exported. As if all these discouragements to exports were not enough, the French government does not allow the French exporter to keep the dollars he has made from his export sales or to convert them freely. He must turn 99 per cent of his dollar proceeds over to the government. And he must turn them over at the official rate.

It is hardly surprising, in the face of such regulations, that in most European countries there is a *chronic* excess of imports over exports. It is hardly surprising that these countries now buy more than they sell. This trade deficit does not prove, however, as Secretary Marshall's Harvard speech and the report of the sixteen nations assume, that Europe's "requirements" are this much greater than "her present ability to pay." It was not primarily brought about by the destructions of war. This chronic excess of imports is being brought about, on the contrary, by Europe's own governmental policies. It is being financed today mainly by American governmental loans. It will continue as long as those loans continue, and as long as the internal policies responsible for it continue.

*   *   *

There will be no long-term economic stability and no real freedom of international trade until nations go back to the gold standard. But the first step toward the resumption of free and normal international trade is the removal of all prohibitions on the rate at which the existing paper currency is bought and sold, either in terms of gold or of other currencies.

*   *   *

For the purpose of making loans or grants to European governments, we have (surviving the now defunct Lend-lease and UNRRA), the Export-Import Bank, the Commodity Credit Corporation, the International Monetary Fund and the International Bank for Reconstruction and Development. In addition, the Treasury Department has acted as the agency to administer the loan to Great Britain. That ought to be about enough government foreign lending agencies without thinking up still another.

Of the two international institutions, the Fund in its present form ought not to exist at all. Its managers are virtually without the power to insist on internal fiscal or economic reforms before they grant their credits. A $25,000,000 credit granted by the Fund to France, for example, is being used to keep the franc far above its real purchasing power and at a level which encourages imports and discourages exports. This merely prolongs the unbalance of French trade and creates a need for still more loans. Such a use of the resources of the Fund not only fails to do any good, but does positive harm.

The International Bank also lacks clear power to insist on reforms. As distinguished from the Fund, however, it at least has power to refuse loans unless the borrower is "in position to meet its obligations."

26

Collapse of a System*
November 21, 1967

The devaluation of the British pound from $2.80 to
$2.40 is not only another declaration of bankruptcy
by Great Britain; it is another revelation of the
bankruptcy of the international money system con-
cocted at Bretton Woods, N.H., in 1944.

The argument put forward by the sponsors of that
system was that if would promote international trade
and domestic prosperity by stabilizing the values of
national currencies and maintaining fixed and
dependable exchange ratios between them. All that
was necessary, they blandly explained, was to make
one key currency—the American dollar—directly
convertible into gold. All the others could simply be
tied to each other by being tied to the dollar. Then
every currency would support all the others, and
everything would be just dandy.

What has been the result? The British pound,
which had already been devalued from $4.86 to $4.03
when it entered the International Monetary Fund,
was devalued again, in September, 1949, from $4.03

*Reprinted by permission of the Los Angeles Times Syndicate.

to $2.80. That action touched off 25 more devaluations of other currencies within a single week.

Since the fund opened for business, in fact, there is hardly one of its hundred or more member currencies, with the exception of the dollar, that has not been devalued at least once. Even before Nov. 18 every currency, without exception, bought less than it did when the fund started. The new devaluation of the pound to $2.40 has already touched off a series of more devaluation of other currencies. Not until at least several months from now will we know how seriously the world monetary edifice has been shaken.

And yet throughout the last 20 years we have been hearing and reading from official sources nothing but endlessly repeated statements about how "successfully" the fund system has been functioning. Only this fall the fund members triumphantly announced a new gimmick, "special drawing rights," to make the system still more successful. These special drawing rights are nothing more than a new form of paper money or paper credit designed to make possible a further uniform international inflation and monetary depreciation that will not show up in the quoted exchange values of individual currencies.

At least an open devaluation of an individual currency, like that of the pound to $2.40, lets us see just who is being swindled and by how much. The first losers are the central banks, private banks and firms and individuals all over the world who trusted the British government's solemn pledges that the pound would not again be devalued.

Maybe some of the "new economists" (though I doubt it) will at last begin asking themselves whether the international gold standard may have had some advantages that they could have overlooked.

Another bankruptcy that the new devaluation emphasizes is the welfare state. Prime Minister Harold Wilson fatuously blames "the speculators," but the real cause of the pound's new downfall is the attempt of Britain to live beyond its means—the cradle-to-grave security, the deficits of the socialized industries, all financed by budget deficits and the printing of more money.

Of course, the devaluation of the pound will bring tremendous pressure on the dollar. The Johnson Administration's ability and will to deal with this are more than questionable. The President has reaffirmed "unequivocally the commitment of the United States to buy and sell gold at the existing price of $35 an ounce." This is all very well as far as it goes. But if this commitment is to be kept, the government will have to slash billions off the Great Society welfare spending and stop the swelling deficit and the constant increase in the paper money supply.

Mr. Johnson has still given no sign that he seriously means to do anything in this direction.

27

The Coming Monetary Collapse*
March 23, 1969

The international monetary system set up at Bretton Woods in 1944 is on the verge of breaking down.

It could still be saved by heroic measures, especially if these were taken in the United States. They would include an immediate slash in projected government expenditures, an immediate balancing of the budget, and a halt in any further increase in the stock of money.

But in the present political and ideological atmosphere, these measures are in the highest degree unlikely.

Parallel measures are even more unlikely in Britain or in France. The Labor government in Britain will never give up its socialistic obsessions. Charles de Gaulle is caught in a chronic dilemma of either yielding to untenable wage demands or having his country paralyzed by strikes.

And nearly every other country, in varying degree, now operates on the fixed assumption that at least some inflation, some constant increase in its stock of paper money, is necessary to prevent an economic slowdown or setback.

*Reprinted by permission of the Los Angeles Times Syndicate.

In this situation, with a constantly increasing amount of irredeemable paper currency, an increasing distrust of that currency, and a diminishing stock of American holdings of gold, it seems likely that one of these days the United States will be openly forced to refuse to pay out any more of its gold at $35 an ounce even to foreign central banks.

We have been getting ever closer to that point. Our Treasury gold stock fell from $22.8 billion at the end of 1957 to $12.4 billion at the end of 1967 and then to $10.367 billion in the week ended June 12, 1968. It has remained at exactly that figure, week after week, since then.

This would simply not be possible, with confidence in the dollar as shaky as it is today (with $13.7 billion American short-term liabilities to foreign banks alone, not to speak of $20.1 billion more such liabilities to other foreigners), if gold were in fact being freely paid out on demand to foreign central banks wanting it and legally entitled to demand it.

It is true that at least up to the end of January a little less than $500 million additional gold was in our exchange stabilization fund, but even the changes in this figure since last March, when the two-price system for gold was adopted, have been practically negligible.

The time must come when even the thin fiction of maintaining the convertibility of the dollar into gold at $35 an ounce will end.

It is most likely to end in the midst of some run or crisis in the foreign exchange market. If it does, and even token gold-convertibility ends, the consequences for the United States and the world will be grave. Currencies would begin fluctuating wildly in terms of each other, and there would be no fixed yardstick or benchmark against which to measure the depreciation of any of them.

It is devoutly to be hoped, therefore, that the moment our government does openly cease to keep the dollar convertible into gold at $35 an ounce, it will at least simultaneously repeal all prohibitions on the buying, selling, or holding of gold by its own citizens. This would not only enable private individuals to protect themselves against further depreciation of paper dollars, but it would lead to gold becoming once more a *de facto* international medium of exchange, and it would greatly mitigate the harm done until a new international gold standard could be officially established.

The complete and acknowledged suspension of gold convertibility is the grim outlook we face if our Treasury officials and monetary managers complacently continue to inflate while pretending that nothing very serious is happening to the dollar.

28

World Inflation Factory*

August, 1971

The latest crisis in the foreign exchanges illustrates once more the inherent unsoundness of the International Monetary Fund system. That should have been obvious when it was first set up at Bretton Woods, N.H., in 1944. The system not only permits and encourages but almost compels world inflation.

There follows a reprint of the article I wrote in *Newsweek* of October 3, 1949, at the time of another major world monetary crisis. I do this to emphasize that today's crisis could have been predicted twenty years ago. It is not merely the result of mistakes in the recent economic and monetary policies of individual nations, but a consequence of the inherently inflationary institutions set up in 1944 under the leadership of Lord Keynes of England and Harry Dexter White of the United States.

In an epilogue I discuss the measures needed to extricate ourselves from the present international monetary crisis and to prevent a repetition.

*Reprinted by permission from *The Freeman*, Foundation for Economic Education, Irvington-On-Hudson, New York.

The World Monetary Earthquake*

Within a single week 25 nations have deliberately slashed the values of their currencies. Nothing quite comparable with this has ever happened before in the history of the world.

This world monetary earthquake will carry many lessons. It ought to destroy forever the superstitious modern faith in the wisdom of governmental economic planners and monetary managers. This sudden and violent reversal proves that the monetary bureaucrats did not understand what they were doing in the preceding five years. Unfortunately, it gives no good ground for supposing that they understand what they are doing now.

This column has been insisting for years, with perhaps tiresome reiteration, on the evil consequences of overvalued currencies. On Dec. 18, 1946, the International Monetary Fund contended that the trade deficits of European countries "would not be appreciably narrowed by changes in their currency parities." I wrote in *Newsweek* of March 3, 1947: "It is precisely because their currencies are ridiculously

160

overvalued that the imports of these countries are overencouraged and their export industries cannot get started." In the issue of Sept. 8, 1947, as well as in my book, *Will Dollars Save the World?* I wrote: "Nearly every currency in the world (with a few exceptions like the Swiss franc) is overvalued in terms of the dollar. It is precisely this overvaluation which brings about the so-called dollar scarcity."

Yet until Sept. 18 of this year the European bureaucrats continued to insist that their currencies were not overvalued and that even if they were this had nothing to do, or negligibly little to do, with their trade deficits and the "dollar shortage" that they continued to blame on America. And the tragedy was that former Secretary of State Marshall, the President, and Congress completely misunderstanding the real situation, accepted this European theory and poured billions of the American taxpayers' dollars into the hands of European governments to finance the trade deficits that they themselves were bringing about by their socialism and exchange controls with overvalued currencies.

In time the managers of the Monetary Fund learned half the lesson. They recognized that most European currencies were overvalued. They recognized that this overvaluation was a real factor in causing the so-called "dollar shortage" and unbalancing and choking world trade. But they proposed the wrong cure.

They did not ask for the simple abolition of exchange controls. (Their own organization in its very origin was tied up with the maintenance of exchange controls.) They proposed instead that official currency valuations be made "realistic." But the only "realistic" currency valuation (as long as a currency is not made freely convertible into a definite weight of gold) is the valuation that a free market would place upon it. Free-market rates are the only rates that keep demand and supply constantly in balance. They are the only rates that permit full and free convertibility of paper currencies into each other at all times.

Sir Stafford Cripps fought to the last against the idea that the rate of the pound had anything to do with the deepening British crisis. Trying to look and talk as much like God as possible, he dismissed all such contentions with celestial disdain. But at the eleventh hour he underwent an intellectual conversion that was almost appallingly complete. We "must try and create conditions," he said, "in which the sterling area is not prevented from earning the dollars we need. This change in the rate of exchange is one of those conditions *and the most important one"* (my italics). And on the theory that what's worth doing is worth overdoing, he slashed the par value of the pound overnight from $4.03 to $2.80.

There are strong reasons (which space does not permit me to spell out at this time) for concluding that the new pound parity he adopted was well below what the real free-market level of widely usable sterling was or would have been on the day he made the change. What he did, in other words, was not merely to adjust the pound to its market value as of Sept. 18 but to make a real devaluation.

The first consequence was to let loose a world scramble for competitive devaluation far beyond anything witnessed in the '30's.

Most nations fixed new rates lower than their existing real price and cost levels called for. These countries, therefore, will now undergo still another epidemic of suppressed inflation. Their internal

162

prices and living costs will start to soar. Unions will strike for higher wages. And if the past (or Sir Stafford's Sept. 18 talk) is any guide, the governments will try to combat this by more internal price-fixing and rationing, continued or increased food subsidies, unbalanced budgets, and wage fixing.

In this country, on the contrary, the tendency will be to drag down our price level somewhat by lowering the dollar price of imported commodities and forcing reductions in the dollar price of export commodities. This will increase our problems at a time when the unions are pressing for a wage increase in the camouflaged form of insurance-pension benefits.

It will be necessary to re-examine our whole foreign economic policy in the light of the new exchange rates. Marshall-plan aid with overvalued European currencies was largely futile; Marshall-plan aid with undervalued European currencies should be unnecessary. In fact, we may soon witness the reversal of the world flow of gold. For the first time since 1933 (if we omit the war years 1944 and 1945) gold may move away from, instead of toward, our shores.

But getting rid of overvalued currencies, even in the wrong way, is nonetheless a tremendous gain. The chief barrier that has held up a two-way flow of world trade in the last five years has at last been broken. The chief excuses for maintaining the strangling worldwide network of trade restrictions and controls have at last been destroyed. Were it not for the echoes of the atomic explosion in Russia, the outlook for world economic freedom would at last be brighter.

The best British comment I have read since the devaluation comes from *The London Daily Express:* "Let every foreign country pay what it thinks the pound is worth...But the socialists will never consent to free the pound. It would mean abandonment of their system of controls...If you set money free you set the people free."

Epilogue 1971

The prediction made in this 1949 piece, that the flow of gold would be reversed, proved correct. The deficit in our balance of payments, in fact, began in 1950. Our 1949 gold stock of nearly $25 billion proved to be its high point. Thereafter it declined. The decline accelerated after 1957 when our balance-of-payments deficits started to reach major proportions.

But all this should not have been too difficult to predict. For on top of the great world realignment of currency values in 1949, our monetary authorities began to inflate our own currency at a greatly increased rate. The dollar "shortage" disappeared, and was soon succeeded by a dollar flood. What would otherwise have been a slight tendency for our prices to fall was offset by an expansion of our money supply. In September, 1947, two years before the 1949 crisis, the U.S. money stock (currency in the hands of the public plus demand bank deposits) was $111.9 billion. In September, 1949, it was only $110 billion. But by December 1950 it had reached $115.2 billion, and by December, 1951, $122 billion. The figure at the end of May, 1971, was $225 billion.

It is important to remember that the present world monetary system is not a natural growth, like the old international gold standard, but an arbitrary scheme devised by a handful of monetary bureaucrats who did not even agree with each other. Some of them wanted inconvertible paper currencies free to fluc-

164

tuate in the foreign exchange markets and "managed" by each country's own bureaucrats solely in accordance with "the needs of the domestic economy." Others wanted "exchange stability," which meant fixed values for each currency in relation to the others. But none of them wanted constant convertibility of his country's currency by any holder into a fixed weight of gold on demand. That had been the essence of the classic gold standard.

So a compromise was adopted. The American dollar alone was to be convertible into a fixed amount (one thirty-fifth of an ounce) of gold on demand. But only on the demand of official central banks, not of private holders of dollars. In fact, private citizens were forbidden to ask for or even to own gold. Then every other nation but the U.S. was to fix a "par value" of its currency unit in terms of the dollar; and it was to maintain this fixed value by agreeing either to buy or sell dollars to whatever extent necessary to maintain its currency in the market within 1 percent of its parity.

The Burden of Responsibility

Thus there was devised a system which appeared to "stabilize" all currencies by tying them up at fixed rates to each other—and even indirectly, through the dollar, tying them at a fixed ratio to gold. This system seemed to have also the great virtue of "economizing" gold. If you could not call it a gold standard, you could at least call it a gold-exchange standard, or a dollar-exchange standard.

But the system, precisely because it "economized reserves," also permitted an enormous inflationary expansion in the supply of nearly all currencies. Even this expansion might have had a definite limit if the

U.S. monetary managers had constantly recognized the awesome burdens and responsibilities that the system put upon the dollar. Other countries could go on inflationary sprees without hurting anybody but themselves; but the new system assumed that the American managers, at least, must always stay sober. They would refrain from anything but the most moderate expansion to keep the dollar constantly convertible into gold.

But the system was not such as to keep the managers responsible. Under the old gold standard, if a country over-expanded its money and credit and pushed down interest rates, it immediately began to lose gold. This forced it to raise interest rates again and contract its currency and credit. A "deficit in the balance of payments" was quickly and almost automatically corrected. The debtor country lost what the creditor country gained.

Just Print Another Billion

But under the gold-exchange or dollar standard, the debtor country does not lose what the creditor country gains. If the U.S. owes $1 billion to West Germany, it simply ships over a billion paper dollars. The U.S. loses nothing, because in effect it either prints the billion dollars or replaces those shipped by printing another billion dollars. The German Bundesbank then uses these paper dollars, these American I.O.U.'s, as "reserves" against which it can issue more D-marks.

This "gold-exchange" system began to grow up in 1920 and 1921. But the Bretton Woods agreements of 1944 made things much worse. Under these agreements each country pledged itself to accept other countries' currencies at par. When holders of

166

dollars shipped them into Germany, the Bundesbank *had* to buy them up to any amount at par with D-marks. Germany could do this, in effect, by printing more paper marks to buy more paper dollars. The transaction increased both Germany's "reserves" and its domestic currency supply.

So while our monetary authorities were boasting that the American inflation was at least less than some inflations in Europe and elsewhere, they forgot that some of these foreign inflations were at least in part the result of our own inflation. Part of the dollars we were printing were not pushing up our own prices at home because they went abroad and pushed up prices abroad.

The IMF system, in brief, has been at least partly responsible for the world inflation of the last twenty-five years, with its increasingly ominous economic, political, and moral consequences.

What Should be Done Now?

As long as the world's currencies continue to consist of inconvertible paper there is no point in setting new fixed parities for them. What is a "realistic" rate for any currency today (in terms of others) will be an unrealistic one tomorrow, because each country will be inflating at a different rate.

The first step to be taken is the one that West Germany and a few others have already taken. No country should any longer be obliged to keep its currency at par by the device of buying and selling the dollar or any other paper currency at par. Paper currencies should be allowed to "float," with their prices determined by supply and demand on the market. This will tend to keep them always "in equilibrium," and the market will daily show which currencies are getting stronger and which are getting weaker. The daily changes in prices will serve as early warning signals both to the nationals of each country and to the managers.

Floating rates will be to some extent disorderly and unsettling; but they will be much less so in the long run than pegged rates supported by secret government buying and selling operations. Floating rates, would moreover, most likely prove a transitional system. It is unlikely that the businessmen of any major nation will long tolerate a paper money fluctuating in value daily.

The next monetary reform step should be for the central banks of all countries to agree at least not to add further to their holdings of paper dollars, pounds, or other "reserve" currencies.

Let Citizens Own Gold

The next step applies to the U.S. alone. There appears to be no alternative now to our government doing frankly and *de jure* what for the last three years it has been doing without acknowledgment but *de facto*: it should openly announce that it can no longer undertake to convert dollars into gold at $35 an ounce. It owns only about $1 in gold for every $45 paper dollars outstanding. Its dollar obligations to foreign central banks alone are now more than twice its holdings of gold. It if really allowed free conversion it would be bailed out of its remaining gold holdings within a week.

The government should also announce that until further notice it will neither buy nor sell gold.

Simultaneously, however, the United States should repeal all prohibitions against its citizens owning, buying, selling, or making contracts in gold. This

168

would mean the restoration of a really free gold market here. Incidentally, because of distrust of floating paper currencies, it would mean that international trade and investment would soon be increasingly conducted in terms of gold, with a weight of gold as the unit of account. Gold, even if not "monetized" by any government, would become an international money, if not *the* international money. On the foreign-exchange markets national paper currencies would be quoted in terms of gold. Even if there were no formal international agreement, this would prepare the way for the return of national currencies, country by country, to a gold standard.

Stop the Reckless Government Spending that Brings Inflation

All this concerns technique. What chiefly matters is national economic and monetary policy. What is essential is that the inflation in the U.S. and elsewhere be brought to a halt. Government spending must be slashed; the budget must be consistently balanced; monetary managers as well as private banks must be deprived of the power of constantly and recklessly increasing the money supply.

Only abstention from inflating can make a gold standard workable; but a gold standard, in turn, provides the indispensable discipline to enforce abstention from inflating.

David Ricardo summed up this reciprocal relation more than 160 years ago:

Though it [paper money] has no intrinsic value, yet, by limiting its quantity, its value in exchange is as great as an equal denomination of coin, or of bullion in that coin....

169

Experience, however, shows that neither a state nor a bank ever has had the unrestricted power of issuing paper money without abusing that power; in all states, therefore, the issue of paper money ought to be under some check and control; and none seems so proper for that purpose as that of subjecting the issuers of paper money to the obligation of paying their notes either in gold coin or bullion.

29

What Must We Do Now?

1983

This concludes our 40-year history of inflation, from the fateful conference at Bretton Woods to the present. What lessons does it teach us? What must we do about it now?

The short answer to these questions is obvious. *We must stop inflating.* But the details of this answer can be complicated, and the political obstacles to getting it done are all but insurmountable.

Let us begin by making a few points clear. Inflation is not some great natural disaster, that falls upon us from without like an earthquake, a volcanic eruption, or a flood. Neither is it some economic accident that is nobody's fault. It is something we bring about by our own actions. If we wish to narrow the blame, we may say that it is something brought about by the actions of our politicians, our government officeholders. But our politicians act as they do because they want to be elected or re-elected. They are responding to the demands, or the presumed demands, of the majority of voters.

It is always very easy to start an inflation, but the longer it has lasted, and the further it has been allowed to progress, the more difficult it becomes to stop.

The cycle begins, say, when the politicians in power decide to confer special benefits on favored groups. The government sets up, for example, an elaborate Social Security system, to guarantee everybody enough to retire on after the age of 65. It initiates a system of unemployment insurance which begins making payments automatically, for 15 weeks, say, to anybody who has quit or been thrown out of work. It offers relief payments, or issues food stamps, to people assumed to be in need "through no fault of their own." It offers subsidies to farmers for growing less. When surplus milk production reduces farm income, the politicians set a minimum price for milk and order the government to buy whatever amount is necessary to maintain that price. The government puts this in storage, in the form of butter or cheese, and when the amount in storage becomes appallingly high, starts giving it away. The politicians provide a score of other handouts or subsidies. And all these programs are justified as the minimum duty of a "compassionate" government.

At first the politicians pay for all these benefits by raising taxes, but this becomes increasingly unpopular. The politicians begin to run out of ideas for additional types of subsidies, so they increase the subsidies they have already established. Social Security benefit payments are increased. Unemployment insurance entitlements are raised, extended to 26 weeks, and sometimes to 39. Relief payments, food stamps, and other subsidies also mount.

Much of this growth is generated by the programs themselves. Social Security causes more and more people to retire early. Unemployment insurance prolongs unemployment. Minimum prices for milk increase the output of milk. And so on.

173

It becomes increasingly difficult, politically and economically, to impose still heavier taxes. The recipients of subsidies and other handouts come to regard them as a right. Any proposal for the slightest reduction is treated as outrageous. No politician dares suggest reducing any subsidy, much less halting it. "Entitlements" grow. Budgets become unbalanced and stay unbalanced. The government pays for the deficits by going further into debt or prints more and more inconvertible paper money.

To be specific, the United States government has not balanced its budget since the fiscal year 1969. Though the tax burden has steadily mounted, there have been 45 deficits in the 53 years since 1930. These deficits have been growing at an accelerative rate. President Reagan—even on the assumption that the cutbacks and freezes in spending proposed in his budget message of Jan. 31, 1983, will be adopted—projected a deficit of $188.8 billion in the fiscal year 1984, $194 billion in fiscal 1985, $148 billion in 1986, $142 billion in 1987, and $117 billion in 1988. When one considers that future budget deficits have been chronically underestimated in the past, the outlook at the moment of writing this is frightening.

The candid recognition of this outlook clearly tells us what must now be done. Congress and the Administration must stop the deficit spending. They must begin not in some indefinite future, but at the earliest possible moment.

Is this asking for the "politically impossible"? We can't say. But what we can say is that if it is not done very soon the consequences will be economically disastrous.

The public, the bulk of the press, and the politicians are unduly complacent at the moment because they have been looking backward instead of forward. What they see is that "the rate of inflation", as they call it (by which they mean the rise in "the price level"), has slowed down in the last few years (from the 13.3 percent in 1979 to 3.9 percent in 1982.) But this has been brought about by causes that can change at any moment. Bad as inflationary conditions have been in the United States, for example, they have been much worse in many other countries. The result is that the dollar, even since we have been off the gold standard, has remained the world's principal "reserve currency." The greater distrust of other currencies has increased the world demand for the dollar. But a sudden lack of confidence in the dollar itself could change this situation overnight.

The value of a currency, like the value of stocks and bonds and commodities on the exchanges, is determined by people's beliefs and expectations rather than directly by the objective facts. If a flight *from* the dollar suddenly developed, we could quickly be thrown into a hyper-inflation. Let us hope that our politicians and monetary authorities will begin to act responsibly before that happens. It is far easier to forestall an inflationary panic—a "crack-up boom"—than to stop it once it has started.

I have put first the halting of domestic deficits (by reduction of spending and not by a further increase in the tax burden), and the consequent strict control of further increases in the money supply, as the most urgent of all measures. But close behind it is the need to abolish the inflationary practices and international lending institutions set up by the Bretton Woods Agreements of 1944. While this step may seem less urgent than bringing domestic government spending under control and restricting the issuance of more

175

paper money, it is nonetheless an inseparable part of what must now be done. For as I have emphasized in the preceding pages, the International Monetary Fund, and the pure paper-money basis on which it now rests, not only superimpose a world inflation upon all the individual national inflations, but systematically give these inflations, and the socialistic policies that bring them about, acquiescence and encouragement.

A word must be said at this point about a question that still seems to be little understood, even by most economists. I have put more emphasis on budget deficits, and less on changes in the money supply, than is customary. I recognize, of course, that increases in the money supply are usually the most direct objective cause for the consequent fall in the purchasing power of the monetary unit. But budget deficits are nearly always the chief reason why the quantity of money is increased; and their chronic persistence is the chief cause of the fear of future inflation. But when, as has happened in this country in the last few years, the Federal Reserve refrains from monetizing the deficits as they appear, it obliges the government to sell its bonds in the open market to raise the money to meet the deficits. This in turn forces up interest rates to oppressive levels for private business, and brings recession and unemployment. But because of the present dominance of a strict mechanical quantity theory of money among many economists, the urgency of halting the deficits has been ignored. The result is a dangerous complacency.

One more step is an essential part of the anti-inflation program I have just outlined. The world must return to a gold standard. That standard, as its detractors insist, may have its imperfections, but all these are more than offset by one decisive negative virtue: it takes our money out of the hands of the politicians. As Ludwig von Mises once put it: "The excellence of the gold standard is to be seen in the fact that it renders the determination of the monetary unit's purchasing power independent of the policies of governments and political parties." (The Theory of Money and Credit, 1953.) And to quote once more the words of David Ricardo in 1817:

> "Experience...shows that neither a state nor a bank ever has had the unrestricted power of issuing paper money without abusing that power; in all states, therefore, the issue of paper money ought to be under some check and control; and none seems so proper for that purpose as that of subjecting the issuers of paper money to the obligation of paying their notes either in gold coin or bullion."

In 1983, alas, there are only a comparative handful of economists who recognize this, and almost none of them are in positions of political power. Moreover, as even few of the present supporters of a gold standard recognize, if we assume that we should try to return to the traditional government-managed type of gold standard, the technical problem of returning to it without precipitating a serious deflation or inflation, has never been so difficult as it is today.

When the value of the paper currency unit has totally disappeared, as with the American Continentals in 1780, the French assignats in 1797, and the German mark in 1923, the problem of fixing a new legal ratio between the outstanding paper currency and gold does not arise. The country simply goes back to gold money. But at times in the past—in the United States in 1875 and 1879, and in England in 1925—when a currency that had gone off the gold standard and depreciated was restored to it at its former rate, the restoration was achieved only at the cost of a long and painful deflation. In England, in fact, the restored former level could not be maintained, and England went off gold again in September, 1931, intensifying the world depression already under way.

The problem that we face today in the United States is that of fixing a workable rate of conversion. If we set the "price" of gold in paper dollars too high, we will bring on a further inflation; if we set it too low, we may bring on a serious deflation. We cannot be guided simply by the current world market gold price. This has fluctuated wildly, even from day to day, in the last few years, influenced mainly by changes in speculative expectations about interest rates, and about how long the present inflation will continue and to what heights it will drive paper-dollar prices.

But, given a return of political responsiblity and courage, the problem is not insoluble. If Congress and the Administration announce a determination to return to a gold standard, if they can balance the budget and keep it balanced for a couple of years, if they can stop or very strictly limit the growth of the paper-money issuance for a similar period, the market price of gold will quickly show a tendency to stabilize. The government can set a date for restoring a gold standard and make a reasonably good estimate of a workable and sustainable rate of conversion.

We could of course return to a merely *private* gold

standard, but this is likely to happen only by default, when the paper dollar has become worthless, and millions of Americans have been ruined. I shall abstain from discussing such a possibility.

We have been drawn into considering the whole problem of what we must do to halt the present American and world inflation. Our discussion has carried us much beyond the narrower subject with which this book has concerned itself—the fatal stimulus to world inflation provided by the International Monetary Fund and the whole ideology embodied in the Bretton Woods Agreements of 40 years ago.

Fortunately, this part of the present world inflationary problem is more easily solved than most of the rest. We cannot, of course, abolish the IMF overnight. For one thing, we will meet determined resistance from most of the other members of the United Nations. But we can at least put a termination to our own contributions. We can urge that the Fund be prevented from making any further increase in its enormous net volume of outstanding loans, and start devoting itself to getting repaid. The business of foreign lending can once more be left to private investors, genuinely concerned about the soundness of their loans.

What we are asking of our politicians is not unreasonable: Let them at least stop subsidizing the socialistic programs and inflations of other countries.

INDEX